BARYSHNIKOV

GENNADY SMAKOV

BARYSHNIKOV

FROM RUSSIA TO THE WEST

FARRAR STRAUS GIROUX · NEW YORK

To my son, Kirill,
and to all Baryshnikov's
admirers in Russia who cannot
see him dancing today

Copyright © 1981 by Gennady Smakov
All rights reserved
Published simultaneously in Canada by McGraw-Hill Ryerson Ltd., Toronto
Printed in the United States of America
Designed by Jacqueline Schuman
First edition, 1981

Library of Congress Cataloging in Publication Data
Smakov, Gennady.
  Baryshnikov: from Russia to the West.
  Includes index.
  1. Baryshnikov, Mikhail. 2. Ballet dancers—Russia—Biography.
GV1785.B348S6 1981 792.8′2′0924 [B] 80–26775

◁ MARTHA SWOPE

 # Acknowledgments

Many have helped me during the making of this book. Joseph Brodsky, like *The Sleeping Beauty*'s Lilac Fairy, stood by its crib. Joseph kindly introduced me to my publisher, Roger Straus, editor-in-chief Aaron Asher, and my editor, Pat Strachan, at Farrar, Straus and Giroux. I was immediately made to feel like a member of the family and am very grateful for the special atmosphere of warmth and encouragement that is endemic to this publishing house.

My thanks go to my good friends Elena Tchernichova, Alexander Minz, and Chinko Rafique, who generously shared their recollections about Baryshnikov's Russian period. Alexander Godunov was also a great help in this regard. I also wish to thank Maya Plisetskaya, Natalia Makarova, Dina Makarova, Clive and Patricia Barnes, Rosemary Winckley, and Dominique Nabokov for their respective contributions to the book, as well as my dear friends Alexander and Tatiana Liberman, Sheldon Atlas, Robert and Cathy Weiss, Ludmila Shtern, and Victor Minakov, whose support sustained me in moments of discouragement. I am very grateful to Helen Atlas, William Chalsma, and Polly Beauwin, whose keen command of the English language helped me endure my unequal duel with this stubborn giant, so unlike his Russian fellow, as the manuscript's first draft developed. I am especially indebted to Vera Krassovskaya, the illustrious Russian ballet historian and critic, whose important books and whose letters to me are a perpetual source of knowledge and inspiration.

I wish to express my enormous gratitude to Gina Kovarsky and Pat Strachan, whose combination of dedication, enthusiasm, and skill in working with my manuscript was truly exemplary. I also thank my copy editors, Carmen Gomezplata and Lynn Warshow, for their unflagging attention to detail.

I am very grateful to the many photographers who allowed me to choose from the spectrum of their work, and to Richard Avedon for his kind permission to adorn the back of the book with his magnificent photograph of Baryshnikov as Petrouchka. I thank my mother, Olga

Poliudova-Smakov, for obtaining unique photographs of Baryshnikov's childhood from his family.

My deepest gratitude goes, of course, to Mikhail Baryshnikov, whose unprecedented achievements in ballet inspired and sustained the writing of this book.

Gennady Smakov
New York, New York

Contents

Illustrations

[*For Mikhail Baryshnikov*]

The classical ballet, let's say, is beauty's keep
whose gentle denizens are moated off from feeling
prosaic things by pits filled up with fiddling,
and drawbridges are hoisted up.

In soft imperial plush you wriggle your backside,
as, thighs aflutter at the speed of shorthand,
a pearl who'll never make your sofa shudder
wings out into the garden in one glide.

We see archfiends in dark-brown leotards
and guardian angels in their tutus flaunting vision;
and then the 'standing o' may blow from sleep Elysian
Tchaikovsky and the other smarts.

The classical ballet! The art of better days!
When grog went hissing down with kisses ten a penny,
the cabs were tearing by, we sang hey nonny-nonny,
and if there was a foe, his name was Marshal Ney.

Gold domes were filling eyes of cops with yellow light;
a small plot gave you birth, the nest you lived and died in.
If anything at all went up sky-high then,
it was no railroad bridge but Pavlova in flight.

How splendid late at night, Old Russia worlds apart,
to watch Baryshnikov, his talent still as forceful!
The effort of the calf, the quivering of the torso
rotating round its axis, start

a flight such as the soul has yearned for from the fates,
as old maids cherish dreams while turning into bitches.
And as for where in space and time one's slipper touches,
well, earth is hard all over; try the States.

—*Joseph Brodsky, 1976*
Translated by Alan Myers with the author

BARYSHNIKOV

Introduction

I heard his name for the first time in Leningrad in 1965 from my friend Igor Tchernichov, who was then a leading dancer at the Kirov: "Alexander Ivanovich [Pushkin] has a fantastic new pupil from Riga—Misha Baryshnikov," Igor said.

"A new replacement for Nureyev?" I inquired.

"No, he is more in Soloviev's mold, and seems to be even better—his ability is just unheard-of. Unfortunately, he's rather short and looks like a big baby . . ."

After several other friends at the Kirov confirmed Igor's opinion of Misha's dancing, I asked to be taken to the Vaganova School to watch this young phenomenon. That day Pushkin was teaching in the big rehearsal hall with two huge mirrors, circled by a balcony. "Make a guess who Baryshnikov is," Igor whispered playfully. Pushkin's young subjects were at the barre, exercising; most of them were short and no one really made an impression. But as they began to execute jumps and turns in the middle of the hall, I immediately noticed a frail-looking, fair boy with distant, luminous eyes and sharp features. Not only the rare coordination of his pirouettes and jumps singled him out, but something special in the way he shaped every step—he was both impishly radiant and absolutely serious.

Shortly thereafter, the ballerina Elena Tchernichova, who was then Igor's wife, brought seventeen-year-old Misha to my place for dinner. He was very shy, speaking far less than he listened. One particular detail struck me: from the way he spoke Russian, almost too properly, one would gather that he was a foreigner who had mastered the language. I assumed that his second native tongue was Latvian, but after we knew each other a little better, Misha set me straight. He explained that when he came to Leningrad he began to realize that command of language was considered the key to the quality of one's cultural baggage and suitability by the Russian intelligentsia. This young dancer's aspirations were quite out of the ordinary. My own experience with dancers prompted me to regard them as self-centered people, totally involved in their own demanding field. Misha was different. Our casual meetings at theater premières, at concerts, and at friends' homes developed into a bond based on mutual interest. Though he was a student and I was a twenty-six-year-old critic and professor of European literature at the Leningrad Institute of Theater, Music, and Cinema, I distinctly recall that we spoke less about dancing than about literature, movies, and the other arts. I don't remember that he had close friends among his fellow dance students; he definitely yearned for companionship from the older generation to which I belonged.

Our affinities have grown stronger with the years, erasing the age difference. I cherish his friendship and stand heavily in his debt . . . but this is a book about a great dancer, Mikhail Baryshnikov.

My initial purpose in writing about Baryshnikov was strictly theoretical: using him as a model could certainly cast light on the general question of what contributes to the making of an exemplary dancer. Obviously, training and experience are important elements in a dancer's development, and so my interest in Baryshnikov's makeup necessarily snowballed into a comparative study of Russian and Western dance schools.

Further variations on my intended theme were prompted by my friendship with Misha and the intense interest with which I've followed his career for the last fifteen years. Although I have tried to avoid gossip and nostalgia, talks with Misha, peripheral vignettes, and memories occasionally color the text. Despite my personal involvement, I have not attempted to write a biography. Baryshnikov is at the height of his talent, and a biography always marks, if not the end of a career, its imminent demise.

What follows is a somewhat personal introduction to Baryshnikov's career thus far—glimpses of him and his work that I hope will reveal his artistic development. It is not enough for a dancer to have Baryshnikov's training and his ability to attain perfection. Circumstances, the times, and the milieu that an artist is subjected to also play a part. No doubt this was what Misha had in mind when he said to me: "I don't feel that my career has taken shape from my will. I'm not motivated by frenzied ambition. I don't consider ballet a sacred craft. It's my work, and I do only what I think is necessary. Everything takes its own shape."

Fortune nurtured Baryshnikov from the time of his pre-graduate performance at the Kirov, when, at eighteen, he appeared in the threadbare pas de deux from *Le Corsaire*. For many years the Kirov had had an audience consisting mainly of foreigners, to whom the Kirov ballet was presented as one of Leningrad's sights. In addition to the tourists, there were the balletomanes, the groupies, the ballet freaks, who came, just as in Pushkin's *Eugene Onegin*, "to hiss Phaedra or Cleopatra off the stage." They were spoiled by the feast of classical dance that had gone on blissfully in the Kirov's gilded, blue-velvet hall for more than one hundred years, while outside its walls cataclysms shook Russia. Everyone recognized everyone else, as if all were members of some sort of dance sect that gathered three or four times a week for esoteric assemblages. These balletomanes would not forgive the dancers the smallest fault. They all but eagerly anticipated a faux pas so they could punish with icy silence whoever should offend the ancient temple of Russian Terpsichore. For Petersburgers, the Kirov has long been what La Scala is for Milan's opera lovers, who are well known for being more stirred up over a scandalous flaw than over perfectly sung embellishments.

The Kirov's productions of *The Sleeping Beauty*, *Giselle*, and *Swan Lake*, with their offensively ramshackle sets and costumes, were hardly likely to enthrall anyone. Therefore, people came to see the stars: Natalia Makarova's portrayal of Giselle, Yuri Soloviev's Blue Bird, Alla Osipenko's Lilac Fairy—and sometimes just to catch a single variation or the finale of a ballet. Only miracle workers were capable of bringing down this house.

On the evening of the Kirov's Vaganova School pre-graduate performance in the spring of 1966, the scene was unimaginable. After Baryshnikov's variation from *Le Corsaire*, in which he demonstrated his miraculous grand pirouette—ideally balanced at a right angle to the stage—the cries of "Bravo" seemed to shake the painted vaults of the theater, threatening to fell the chandeliers and crack the layers of gilding. Not quite ten years earlier, the same kind of enthusiasm had greeted Rudolf Nureyev's brilliant graduate performance of the same pas de deux. The animal magnetism that Nureyev's body unleashed had not been seen by the Kirov audience since the time of Vakhtang Chabukiani, the illustrious virtuoso of the thirties. His Tartar temperament imbued Nureyev's dancing with electric energy.

Baryshnikov's image was nothing of the kind. In *Le Corsaire* he looked less like a slave consumed by love than like a young ephebus overflowing with the joy of youth and a somewhat ambivalent sexuality. His main attractions were an almost incredibly pure classical technique combined with infectious charm. Baryshnikov passed lightly and seemingly spontaneously from one movement to another; it was as if his body were composing the choreography on the spot, stripping away the patina of the usual *morceau de virtuosité* seen in performance after performance. Baryshnikov created the rare impression of a body dancing itself, without instructions. His superb coordination, balance, precision, and musicality were inborn, merely polished by training. These qualities can be mimicked with good schooling and constant refinement, but the imitation is never a match for native gifts. Misha's purity of technique recalled Yuri Soloviev, a phenomenal Kirov virtuoso of the sixties, but in artistry Soloviev suffered in comparison.

While Nureyev evoked associations with Chabukiani among the old-timers, an analogy with Vaslav Nijinsky came to mind in Baryshnikov's case. Legends about Nijinsky, his fabled leap across almost the whole of the Maryinsky stage in the *Blue Bird* pas de deux, still stirred the imagination of the Kirov habitués. The legendary name was tossed around the lobby after Baryshnikov's debut, capping off the overwhelming enthusiasm.

In the audience that evening was Elizaveta Time, the first Cléopâtre in Fokine's *Egyptian Nights*, and a living witness to the Russian ballet throughout its years of glory. I asked her whether Baryshnikov's technique and artistry reminded her of Nijinsky. The venerable lady, who had not left her place even during the entr'acte, answered: "You can believe me, my friend, Nijinsky never danced like that and did not possess such devastating charm. In my time, there weren't any virtuosi on a level with Soloviev; it's all talk how they twirled around fifteen pirouettes at a time, and did *entrechats douze*. No one in my memory danced the way this boy dances."

Baryshnikov's career began with the aura of a legend in the making, and that nimbus has surrounded his every subsequent step in Russia and the West.

1 BEGINNINGS

◁ *Le Corsaire*, 1966. First appearance on the Kirov stage

BARYSHNIKOV WAS BORN on January 27, 1948, in Riga, the capital of Latvia. Eisenstein was born and grew up in the same city, and it was from there that Anna Pavlova launched the marathon dance career that would take her all over the world.

Riga is a cosmopolitan blend of Russian and European influences. Architecturally, it combines late Gothic and heavy German styles: Gothic spires stand beside thick-haunched caryatids, Corinthian columns vie with art nouveau ornaments popular in the 1920s, and narrow medieval streets are intersected by wide modern avenues. Ancient trees and the Dvina River lend romantic charm to the city. Leningrad, with its European flavor and classical grid, did not represent as extreme a change for Baryshnikov as it did for Rudolf Nureyev, who grew up in the shapeless Bashkir town of Ufa.

In Riga, Baryshnikov developed an affinity with classical tradition that his move to Leningrad strengthened. Leningrad's architectural classicism may have contributed to Baryshnikov's sense of line and proportion in the classical dance. Indeed, if a city's architecture reflects and shapes the mind of its inhabitants, it is not surprising that Petersburg—not Moscow, with its confusion of architectural styles—was always renowned for its classical dancers.

Baryshnikov is the son of a Soviet officer, Nikolai Baryshnikov, by his second wife, Alexandra Kiseleva (Misha has a half brother and a half sister in Russia). Like the families of most of the Russian stars, the Baryshnikovs had no professional connection to the ballet. Misha discusses his childhood reluctantly even with intimates, quoting instead a phrase of Anna Akhmatova's: "Nothing is more sordid than childhood."

In fact, his childhood was marred by an early tragedy—the separation of his parents. His mother abandoned the family, leaving twelve-year-old Misha in the care of his grandmother and his father. Baryshnikov's mother was a beautiful woman (he has her face) whose remarkable energy could not be fully utilized in a Soviet context. This restless individualism may have contributed to the anguish that led to her desertion. For Misha her loss was a wound that did not heal.

The only images from childhood that he recalls today with joy are of frequent forays into the woods for mushrooms (a beloved Russian pastime), picnics with his parents, and fishing. These expeditions contributed to Baryshnikov's love of the outdoors. In later years he would frequently go to the country to visit friends, but his constant dream of acquiring a place in the country was realized only in America. (There

is probably nowhere Misha feels happier than at his house in Connecticut, a nineteenth-century, stone structure, surrounded by acres of hilly land. Misha's dogs—the black poodle, Goulue, named for the cabaret dancer of Toulouse-Lautrec's day, and the golden retriever, Katia, among them—love to swim in a nearby pond. Baryshnikov plans to spend most of his time at the house when he retires from dancing.)

Misha became interested in ballet at the age of twelve—like Natalia Makarova, largely by chance. He was no "sissy"—quite the contrary, he played soccer with the other boys and was involved in other sports. One day his mother, a ballet lover, took him to audition for the Riga dance school, which was then considered excellent. He was accepted and took a liking to dancing immediately. As a child he'd already fantasized about performing—perhaps as a concert pianist with a large orchestra—so the theatrical atmosphere interested him from the start.

His father looked askance at Misha's infatuation with dance. During the heyday of Russian ballet, to belong to the Imperial Ballet School, which the Tsar and Tsarina often visited, imprinting kisses on the brow of well-behaved pupils, was a great honor. But in the Soviet period, until the mid-fifties, ballet came to be regarded as a frivolous

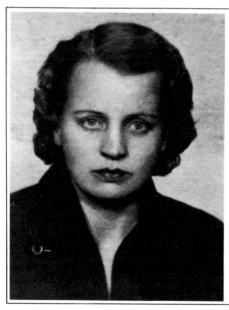

Baryshnikov's mother,
Alexandra Kiseleva

profession, suitable only for girls. Boys were supposed to become engineers, pilots, or shipbuilders.

It was Misha's striking success in ballet that made his father put up with his choice of profession. But real appreciation came only after Baryshnikov's defection. Almost three years later, friends smuggled a copy of *Baryshnikov at Work* (Knopf, 1976) to Nikolai Baryshnikov, fatally ill in Sverdlovsk with a brain disease. The sight of the book seemed to revive a forgotten memory. With tears in his eyes, he turned the pages and suddenly said, quite distinctly: "My little son . . . my pride . . ."

In a sense, Misha's choice was determined by the ideological climate. Baryshnikov's formative years coincided with the period of Khrushchev's thaw in the early sixties. Khrushchev shattered Stalin's image as a benevolent leader by revealing him to be a murderous dictator. For the generation born before or during World War II— mine and that of the poet Joseph Brodsky and the dissident writer Vladimir Bukovsky—the Khrushchev period was a time of reevaluation. Many thirteen-year-olds in our generation had cried at Stalin's funeral in 1953 and were shocked by the revelation of his villainy. In the late fifties and early sixties we sought to retrieve Russia's cultural past, searching under piles of Soviet pulp for slender volumes of Andrei Bely and Nikolai Berdyaev, of Mandelstam, Kuzmin, and Akhmatova, all of whom had been removed from cultural currency. We took a great interest in what had been suppressed for almost forty years: turn-of-the-century Russian poetry, the Russian church, the "World of Art" painters, Diaghilev's ballets, and Russian constructivism in the twenties.

Bukovsky and Brodsky's generation was older than Baryshnikov's only by some eight years, but under the circumstances, that amounted to decades. Stalin's death and the posthumous disclosure of his ruthlessness did not shock Misha as it did us. For him, these events did not signify the downfall of a pantheon of heroes with a seemingly inviolable moral code. But when he reached adolescence in the early sixties, his was an upside-down world devoid of ideals. The members of Bukovsky and Brodsky's generation fought against this ideological deprivation by becoming political dissenters or adopting the moral values of Russian religious philosophy. Misha's generation suffered from the same spiritual vacuum, but they could resist its debilitating influence only by means of a nihilistic sense of irony. Disillusionment prevented young people from mustering much enthusiasm for their careers. Liberal-arts professions became more popular than engineering or shipbuilding, which now seemed devoid of spiritual reward.

Some compromised, repeating the old Russian proverb: "If you live among the wolves, you have to howl with them." Others became inward emigrés, who seemed to take nothing seriously, including career, morality, family, and love. Misha adopted an ironic, self-mocking mask. It was an amusing façade behind which he hid his insecurity and ideological anxieties. Ballet, too, could become an escape and offer him the kind of solace he needed.

It is no accident that from the mid-fifties through the early sixties ballet in Russia again became fashionable among young people as an art that provided a link with the past and as a highly organized, steady microcosm, uninfluenced by political doctrine. Ideologically pure, it was deemed a morally authentic, "sinless" profession. And ballet provided an illusion of stability, a refuge from the unsatisfactory present. For Misha personally, ballet was another way of protecting the inner self. He could master the dance's formal language and hide behind its glittering exterior.

When Baryshnikov was admitted to the Riga dance school in 1960, it occupied the only two large rooms in a small building. Students enrolled in a nine-year ballet curriculum modeled on the Leningrad Vaganova School. They usually started at the age of nine or ten; Misha was twelve. Because of his exceptional abilities, he learned the grammar of classical ballet so fast that in 1962 he was transferred to an advanced class. In addition to the ballet curriculum, students followed an academic program at a nearby school affiliated with the Riga Conservatory of Music. Budding dancers had to fit history, literature, math, piano, French, and art-history lessons into an already busy schedule.

"Every day we ran back and forth between the two schools across the square," recalled Alexander Godunov in an interview. Godunov, who defected to the United States in 1979, was Baryshnikov's classmate in Riga for three years. "Natalia Leontieva taught the beginners' class; in the intermediate and advanced classes Yuris Kapralis took her place. Misha was a wonderboy whose phenomenal physical equipment combined with extreme zest and conscientiousness . . . Misha and I were short boys, always worrying about how we would grow. Someone told us that tomato juice was good for making you grow tall;

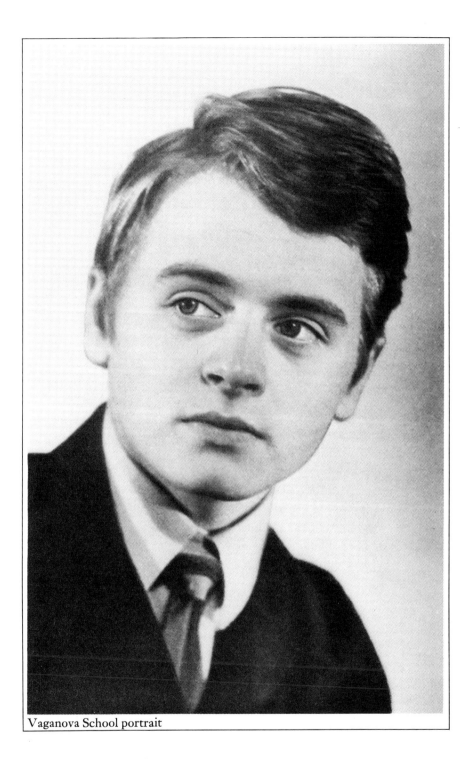
Vaganova School portrait

somebody else told us that sleeping on soft beds would prevent us from reaching our full height. So Misha and I drank tomato juice all the time and took the soft mattresses off our beds and slept on hard boards. We did everything we could to grow tall . . . Later on, our ways parted: in 1964 Misha left for Leningrad to enter the Vaganova School. I followed him, but failed to get into Alexander Pushkin's class for a silly reason. The director of the Vaganova School, Valentin Ivanovich Shelkov, suddenly driven by bureaucratic ardor, demanded a special permit from the Riga dance school which I couldn't obtain. Latvia, as one of the fifteen Soviet republics, nationalistically treasured its young regional talents and didn't want to fill the Kirov or the Bolshoi with them."

Discouraged by Shelkov's refusal, Godunov went to Moscow to pursue his ballet career. Seventeen years later, in 1981, Baryshnikov's and Godunov's paths crossed again at the American Ballet Theatre

when Godunov became a principal dancer under Misha's guidance as artistic director.

In 1974, I happened to be in the same box as Yuris Kapralis, Baryshnikov's former teacher in Riga, at a performance of *Giselle*—one of Baryshnikov's last *Giselles* at the Kirov. Baryshnikov was dancing with Natalia Bessmertnova, a frequent partner of his in those years. During the intermission, we talked about Misha's early training. According to Kapralis, Misha looked like a *demi-caractère* dancer, rather than a *danseur noble*: stocky, with a large head and no big natural spring, but ideally turned-out, musical, and quick to catch on. Baryshnikov was also extremely determined and unwilling to be second-best; his technique improved rapidly.

Any competition between Misha and Alexander Godunov, Kapralis recalls, was merely professional. Godunov looked nothing like the athlete he resembles today. He was short and only shot up later. Both

In Alexander Pushkin's class / PATRICIA BARNES

boys were capable and developed quickly, but Misha was playful and spontaneous, Sasha (Godunov's nickname) more collected and organized. The dance came easily to both of them, though what struck Kapralis as unusual, besides Misha's charm and control, was his cerebral approach.

In September 1964, Misha entered Alexander Ivanovich Pushkin's class at Leningrad's Vaganova School, which was named after the great teacher Agrippina Vaganova. Pushkin was the last of the Russian ballet's glorious pleiad of masters, some of whom had worked with the choreographer Marius Petipa. By the early sixties, the names of such leading teachers as Alexander Shiryaev, Nicolai Ivanovsky, Vladimir Ponomaryov, and Nicolai Soliannikov were surrounded by legend. It was because of their efforts that male virtuosity developed as it did in the Soviet period. They worked with such figures as Alexei Yermolaev, Konstantin Sergeyev, and Vakhtang Chabukiani. The last of this old guard was Pushkin, who by a whim of fate had been passed over in the turmoil and bloodletting of Stalin's day. Baryshnikov came to Pushkin when the Riga dance school was on tour in Leningrad. The younger pupils had been brought along to participate in the performance.

"The moment I arrived in Leningrad, I fell head over heels in love with the place," Baryshnikov recalled in his only interview in Russia, on the occasion of his receiving the title of Honored Artist of the U.S.S.R. "I decided to try my luck at the Vaganova School and was accepted into the seventh-year class given by Alexander Ivanovich Pushkin, with whom I studied for the next three school years."

But the period of Baryshnikov's work and friendship with Pushkin lasted twice that long. Even when he was a soloist with the Kirov, Misha continued to attend Pushkin's professional class, until the teacher's death on March 20, 1970. Pushkin was struck by a heart attack and collapsed on the street. Help was late in arriving and he died in the hospital shortly after at the age of sixty-two.

Studying with Pushkin was significant for Baryshnikov, first of all because the older man commanded an encyclopedic knowledge of the male classical repertoire and was committed to preserving its glorious traditions. Pushkin began to study ballet in the private school of Nikolai Legat, who had taken over the reins of the Maryinsky Theater from the aging hands of Marius Petipa in 1904. There followed, for Pushkin, years of study in the Imperial Ballet Institute on Theater

Street, the school later renamed the Agrippina Vaganova Leningrad Choreographic Institute, better known as the Vaganova School. Pushkin studied with Petipa and Fokine's associates: Alexander Shiryaev (1867–1941), an expert in character dance, and Anna Pavlova's coach; Nicolai Ivanovsky (1893–1961), master of historic-popular dance (antique minuets, the gavotte, etc.); Alexander Monakhov (1884–1945), a specialist in various periods of the ballet and master of pantomime and character dance; and Vladimir Ponomaryov (1892–1951), a virtual encyclopedia of classical dance, and teacher of numerous famous dancers, such as Chabukiani, Sergeyev, and Yermolaev.

Pushkin was principal dancer of the Kirov theater (the Maryinsky, prior to 1934) from 1925 to 1953. He was master of the classical dance, but not a *danseur noble*, though he did dance Siegfried in *Swan Lake*, the Prince in *The Nutcracker*, the Youth in *Les Sylphides*, and Vatslav in *The Fountain of Bakhchisarai*. Famous for his phenomenal natural leap, Pushkin is remembered in the annals of ballet as an amazing Blue Bird in *The Sleeping Beauty*, the Water Spirit from *The Humpbacked Horse*, and Actaeon from *Esmeralda*.

Elena Tchernichova, a former soloist with the Kirov and now ballet master at ABT, recalls Alexander Pushkin as the Blue Bird in *The Sleeping Beauty* in one of his last performances on the Kirov stage with Nina Zheleznova Florina: "It must have been about 1951, because I was a student in the first years at the Vaganova School. At forty-three, he looked like an old man. His knees barely supported him, his belly stuck out, but his soaring jump was still there. The audience was amazed. His ability to jump was almost miraculous—I mean the imperceptible way he got off the stage and landed. He learned that secret from the old masters of the Maryinsky."

Apparently feeling a stronger calling to be a pedagogue than a dancer, the twenty-five-year-old Pushkin began teaching in 1932. From 1953 on, he conducted an advanced class at the Kirov theater. Pushkin's classes, as described by his numerous pupils, were marked by the rare logic of his balletic combinations. He did not give out formulas or detailed explanations of how to execute a movement, and rarely bothered with specific suggestions. Instead, the logic of the combination itself led the body to execute the steps correctly. By methodically training the muscles, Pushkin developed the body's "memory" so that the dancer could execute any combination without thinking about which muscles to put to work. In Pushkin's method, the principles of

Ballet Museum of the Vaganova School, with Balanchine's former colleague Marietta

Frangopulo / N. SLEZINGER

the Russian school were paramount. The emphasis was on equipping the muscles, through a consistent and uniform technique, for every aspect of classical dance.

Pushkin's method also allowed the dancer's individuality to take shape. In the same way that an opera singer inevitably colors a flawlessly performed musical passage with his own individual timbre, velvet or shrill, so a dancer fostered by Pushkin would suffuse movement with his own emotions. Though two dancers may use the same technique and though their muscles may have had identical training, their performances will be emotionally distinct.

Pushkin the pedagogue had another strength. Because of his own natural gift, he was especially good at developing the jump in those to whom it did not come naturally. Rudolf Nureyev's jump, for instance, came as a result of Pushkin's efforts. Misha's jump was already strong, but Pushkin stimulated his natural coordination and so increased the jump's amplitude and height. Elena Tchernichova, who rehearsed *Raymonda* with Pushkin for her graduate performance at the Vaganova School and participated in his advanced class, says: "Pushkin developed the jump, I think, because his logical combinations were short,

At a Leningrad bookstore / N. SLEZINGER

not difficult, and good for coordination. In class, his comments were simple and uncomplicated, like: 'Stretch your leg.' Or: 'Hold in the shoulder.' Many people even had the impression that this was all elementary. But that was Pushkin's secret. His method was especially good for Baryshnikov, since it permitted the dancer to refine his already conditioned body, to train and extend its natural capabilities."

Pushkin had many gifted students in his classes, but, the English dancer Chinko Rafique, who studied with Pushkin at the same time as Baryshnikov, told me, "Misha's receptivity to the dance was unique to the walls of the school and to Pushkin's class. He was like a sponge, soaking up everything, and Alexander Ivanovich only had to give him the slightest direction. I remember clearly his reflection in the mirror, taut, stretching out his leg in an arabesque so that it looked as though his body was extended beyond the limits of natural capacity."

As Baryshnikov says in the Russian interview mentioned earlier: "For me, Pushkin was the standard of professionalism. There are all kinds of teachers: some are kind, almost buddies to the students; others are excessively severe. Pushkin was the golden mean. There was nothing formal about his lessons, nothing showy. He was reserved with the students. When they first came to his class, they would often say: 'What's so special about this?' It was as if everything came of itself. But that was Pushkin's strength. And most important, he had a real relationship with the pupils. Patiently and without pressure, he would bring the student to the idea of self-education. Everyone taught himself under his guidance."

In Misha's profile of Pushkin, "self-education" is a key word. Pushkin became not only a ballet teacher to Baryshnikov but a spiritual teacher as well. He was a member of the nearly extinct pre-revolutionary intelligentsia whose cultural standards became the measure of his pupil's attitude to life, the ballet, and art in general. In Pushkin, Baryshnikov found a mentor who was both effective and unobtrusive.

Pushkin had an old-fashioned manner, exemplified by his unhurried, meticulous Petersburg speech, which brooked no vulgarity or slang, and by his aristocratic way of life. His apartment was filled with old mahogany furniture; there he and his wife, Kseniia Iosifovna Iurgenson, a former ballerina, observed all the rules of Russian hospitality. Later, after the Pushkins' deaths, a divan in the style of the Russian Emperor Paul I, an oval mirror, and other small mementos found their way to Baryshnikov's apartment on the Moika Canal (located not far from the

Hermitage and the Winter Canal, in one of the most picturesque sections of Leningrad).

From 1964 to 1967 Baryshnikov lived with other students in the Vaganova School dormitory, an uncomfortable brick building on Pravda Street, where the young hopefuls were packed ten or more to a room. For him, Pushkin's house gradually became a home away from home. "It was an especially cheery spot," recalls Chinko Rafique, "and we would go there every day after lessons, as if it were home. The door was always open to Pushkin's pupils, who were always hungry.

The Moika Canal, Leningrad
/ N. SLEZINGER

Kseniia Iosifovna always fed us—the food was simple but good: beef stew, bouillon. Then the talk would start." Misha entered Pushkin's life just after Nureyev's defection. According to Rafique, Pushkin was deeply affected by this departure, and to a degree, Misha replaced Rudi in his eyes.

Pushkin inculcated in Misha both a tremendous respect for and an eagerness to absorb Russian culture. Stressing the necessity of professionalism, he encouraged Misha to approach ballet as a job incompatible with cheating. But above all, Baryshnikov most clearly owes his

intellectual curiosity to Pushkin. As an heir to the Russian intelligentsia, he was determined to explore aspects of Western culture from
which Soviet artistic life has for many years been isolated.

Baryshnikov's fervent desire to familiarize himself with both the
Russian cultural past and contemporary Western innovations in art
was unique among his colleagues at the Kirov, who were mostly ig-
norant of or highly indifferent to cultural phenomena. Misha's motto,
often formulated as "It's shameful not to know," expressed his eagerness for learning. William Faulkner and Osip Mandelstam, for example,
immediately became Baryshnikov's favorite authors when they were
belatedly rediscovered in the sixties.

Misha's early receptivity helped him become conscious of the pro-
vinciality of Soviet culture caused by an artificial post-revolutionary
rupture with many great Russian artistic traditions. In the 1960s, when
he had a chance to see the choreography of Balanchine, John Cranko,
and Roland Petit, he did not (unlike most Soviet dancers) find it
difficult to admit that Russian ballet had not kept up with the West.
Many Soviet intellectuals have developed an almost subconscious reaction, a kind of negative inferiority complex which they conceal be-
neath a characteristic Russian intolerance of the achievements of
Western culture. And the stronger the expression of this aggression,
the more obvious its defensive roots. Baryshnikov happily failed to fall
under this corroding influence, resisting an ever-increasing Soviet pro-
vinciality. Baryshnikov's greatest debt to Pushkin—his independence
of mind—would later serve him well in the West.

2 DANCER WITHOUT *EMPLOI*

◁ *Don Quixote*, with Ninel Kurgapkina / BLIOKH

BARYSHNIKOV MADE HIS DEBUT with the Kirov in 1967. Though still the best classical ballet company in the world, it had lost much of its earlier brilliance. The Kirov's decline was the result of its premature enshrinement as a cultural relic and classical dance museum. To understand its story, one must recall that the illustrious theater has long seemed under a curse. It is as if a fate, personified by the Russian bureaucracy, both tsarist and Bolshevik, had determined to take revenge on the temple of classical dancing, which was alien to any political doctrine.

The company had survived as an island of classical art during the cultural upheaval of early-twentieth-century modernism and the political turmoil of revolution. But it had paid an artistic price for such stability. Vigorously resisting change, the Maryinsky-Kirov nurtured classicism at the expense of experimentation. To many Maryinsky-Kirov artists, the theater had become a realm of frozen beauty. Some grew impatient enough with its rigid management to flee. Diaghilev began the exodus when he initiated the Saisons Russes, taking the first "season" of his famous enterprise to Paris in 1909. Anna Pavlova also went on tour, leaving Russia for extensive periods and finally setting out on a worldwide dance tour which lasted until her death in 1931.

In the 1920s, George Balanchine and the ballerinas Alexandra Danilova and Olga Spessivtseva left the theater. Indeed, Western ballet might never have developed to its present state had bureaucratic intransigence not forced major Russian artists to leave their native country.

Some dancers, like Nijinsky and Spessivtseva, found respite from artistic constraints only in madness. The pressure to conform took its toll on others as well, in a sometimes sinister fashion. In 1924, Lidia Ivanova, a promising young ballerina who was Balanchine's partner, drowned. Although the circumstances surrounding the incident are still obscure, some evidence indicates that it was a murder instigated by the KGB. And Yuri Soloviev, famous as an incomparable Blue Bird and Spectre de la Rose, and known for his extraordinary, soaring leap, committed suicide with no obvious motive in 1977.

In the 1930s and '40s the Kirov's best young dancers, such as Galina Ulanova, Marina Semenova, and Alexei Yermolaev, joined the Bolshoi in Moscow (the way to the West was closed). The Kirov took on a secondary status, while the Bolshoi enjoyed the privileges—larger subsidies included—of Party patronage. The Bolshoi's prima ballerinas often married into the party's upper echelons, and the corps was said to be an underground harem for the Secret Police and its notorious director, Lavrenti Beria. Stalin himself had a weakness for this vestige of imperial luxury. He adored Marina Semenova for her marvelous performances of Georgian folk dances, and apparently took pleasure in watching Fokine's Sylphides and Petipa's Nereids.

But the Maryinsky—renamed the Kirov in 1935 after a Party leader whose murder was a pretext for Stalin's Great Terror of 1937–39—quietly continued to uphold the St. Petersburg dance tradition through the fifties. Under close supervision of the Party bureaucracy, *Swan Lakes* and *Sleeping Beauties* flourished. The company looked askance at the Bolshoi's less meticulous, more extravagant style, though the latter was soon to take Western audiences by storm.

The Kirov's devotion to tradition was well served in the mid-fifties and between 1960 and 1970 by its powerful choreographic director Konstantin Sergeyev. But Sergeyev's aesthetic vision was limited, and when Baryshnikov made his debut, a decade of Sergeyev's management had already severely hindered the company's development. Sergeyev was an absolutist who single-handedly determined the Kirov's repertoire. As a disciple of Ponomaryov's, he was well schooled in the Petersburg dance tradition; Petipa's style ran in his blood, and he could flawlessly restage the old Petipa ballets. But on the contemporary front, Sergeyev was undiscerning.

During the Stalinist period, a new form emerged in Soviet ballet—the "drama ballet," a full-length production with relatively little dancing, inflated with pantomime to illustrate the twists of plot. Other features—frequent crowd scenes and a reliance on visual effects—still prevail today, especially in the Bolshoi's repertoire. The drama ballet evolved in the late twenties and early thirties as a lavish vehicle for celebrating the state.

These works differed only in their plots, borrowed from Pushkin (*The Bronze Horseman*) or Shakespeare (*Othello* and *Romeo and Juliet*), or based on the formulas of socialist realism. The latter focused on social conflicts and various aspects of the class struggle. *The Red Poppy* (1927) dramatized the plight of Chinese coolies, using the love story of a poor Chinese barroom dancer and a Soviet captain as background. *The Flames of Paris* (1932) glorified the peasant heroes of the French Revolution. Other subjects included the problems of Soviet collective existence (*The Bright Stream*, 1935), and dangers presented by class enemies—Western spies, for instance, as in *Svetlana* (1939). These pseudo-ballets are notable only in that they influenced the direction of Sergeyev's artistic policy at the Kirov.

Sergeyev's own choreography fell into the socialist-realist mold. He created unimaginative, politically didactic works that contributed little to the repertoire. *The Path of Thunder*, for example, based on South African writer Peter Abrahams's novel about apartheid, or *The Distant Planet*, a ballet about man in space, a popular theme after Yuri Gagarin's first flight, were banal and unsophisticated. Similarly forgettable works by other choreographers found their way into the repertoire, like Rostislav Zakharov's *"Russia" Has Come into Port*, which pitted virtuous Russian sailors against their corrupt Western counterparts. Years of rehearsals and the energy of the world's best dancers were thus squandered. For all his professionalism, Sergeyev could not see these works for what they were.

His blind spot endeared him to the authorities and ensured his staying power. His ballets never endangered the doctrine of socialist realism, which was, in fact, a means of flattering Party chiefs in a form comprehensible to them. But despite the security of his position, Sergeyev was jealous of dancers who might threaten his preeminence. He had been an unrivaled *danseur noble* in his prime, and refused to confer that position on a young successor. So when Nikita Dolgushin emerged as the likely heir in 1958, Sergeyev countered. Dolgushin, an ideal Romantic dancer, had created a sensation as Albrecht to Natalia Makarova's Giselle. After his debut in *Giselle*, it was said that a new Sergeyev had appeared. Feya Balabina, a former prima ballerina and Sergeyev's first wife, was so moved by Nikita's performance that she went backstage, weeping, to kiss his hands. She maintained that he was the very image of Sergeyev.

Such talk provoked Sergeyev's jealousy. He spread rumors that Nikita was psychologically unstable and professionally unreliable. As a result, Nikita was given smaller parts and classical *pas de trois* which wasted his artistic potential. A discouraged Nikita left Leningrad for Novosibirsk, which is provincial by comparison, and his career never recovered from Sergeyev's blow.

Sergeyev tenaciously held on to the reins, and by 1967 few Kirov members gave much thought to creativity. Most concentrated on ways to get selected for the next foreign tour—the only financial break available to a dancer, whose average salary was roughly $200 per month. The dancers received only 10–15 percent of their foreign earnings—the Soviet government kept the rest—but by economizing carefully, they could sometimes afford a car. (Cars, most of them Soviet-made, are more readily obtainable in the U.S.S.R. with foreign currency.) Dancers would also bring back items worth a fortune on the black market, like jeans, mohair jackets, lingerie, and footwear, which would enable them to buy cooperative apartments. A change in living conditions was often sorely needed, since many dancers, even stars, lived in tiny studios or shared small apartments with their parents, to the detriment of all concerned. Natalia Makarova and her second husband, a successful film director, Alexei Kvanihidze, lived for three years in a minuscule room the size of a big walk-in closet, with barely space for a bed and a ceiling-high pile of suitcases. (Things weren't much better at the Bolshoi; until 1959 its *ballerina assoluta* Maya Plisetskaya lived in a huge communal apartment in Moscow. It housed twenty families, who shared two baths.)

Trips abroad began to seem like necessities. A dancer was selected not only for talent but for ideological loyalty (few risked even telling a subversive joke). It also helped to be on good terms with the local authorities—Sergeyev and Peter Rachinsky, the Kirov's supervising director. Every candidate was observed tirelessly by the KGB and by other dancers acting as informants. Intrigue and secrecy were rife. As a ballerina said to me in 1968: "Nobody does anything but lie and everybody fears everybody else, just as under Stalin." The list of those under consideration by the special commission of the KGB was not revealed until the day of departure, but even dancers whose names appeared on the final list relaxed only when the plane was off the ground and last-minute changes were impossible.

Intensive preparation preceded each trip. Ballets scheduled for the tour were rehearsed more often than regular performances. Worse, according to Alexander Minz, a former Kirov dancer, and a principal with ABT, the tours had a negative effect on the creative atmosphere at the theater during the late fifties and early sixties. Sergeyev took advantage of the charged, competitive climate to consolidate his position. The lack of trust among company members and the intricacies of Kirov politics caused Baryshnikov, young and vulnerable when he joined the company, to perfect his impenetrable mask. He retreated into himself, becoming secretive like everyone else, even with friends.

But Sergeyev looked favorably on Baryshnikov, knowing that

Misha's talent could enhance his own choreography. At the time, Sergeyev hoped to cast Baryshnikov or Valery Panov (who, in 1974, also left Russia) as Hamlet. And since Baryshnikov could not be called a *danseur noble*—his *emploi* did not fit one specific category— Sergeyev had no cause for jealousy.

Baryshnikov, in fact, presented something of a problem, because he could not easily be cast into any line of balletic *emploi*, about which Kirov regulations were strict. A dancer's physical appearance, not only his technical capabilities, led to his use as either a *danseur noble* or a *demi-caractère*. Musculature also played a decisive role. Softly curving, longish "Apollonian" muscles indicated a lyrical-romantic *emploi*. A "Herculean" build with more prominent muscles would put the dancer into the heroic repertoire.

The same was true for ballerinas. Those known for their flowing line and fluid hands were permitted to dance *Swan Lake*, but rarely *Giselle*. The latter demanded soaring leaps and independent, expressive hands. Irina Kolpakova danced Giselle but never Odette; Alla Osipenko was a superb Odette but never a Giselle. *Emploi* was thought to preserve the integrity of a ballet style, whether Romantic (*Giselle* and *Les Sylphides*) or "classical" (Marius Petipa's *Swan Lake*, *La Bayadère*, *The Sleeping Beauty*).

At the Bolshoi, these rules were treated comparatively nonchalantly. True, Maya Plisetskaya, an incomparable Odette, never danced Giselle (which would have been miscasting), but she did appear as *The Sleeping Beauty*'s Aurora, though her unique gifts and the particular demands of the role were incompatible. At the Bolshoi, the soubrette Ekaterina Maximova appeared in *Swan Lake*, the romantic ballerina Natalia Bessmertnova as Kitri, but such liberties were impossible at the Kirov. Konstantin Sergeyev, who'd been the ideal *danseur noble*, was especially careful in enforcing the restrictions of *emploi*. He upheld Petipa's principle that mastery ought to be revealed within specific stylistic confines. The narrower they were, the greater the challenge and the more effective the result.

The specifications for men were strictly defined. *Danseurs nobles* must be tall, have large facial features, broad shoulders, long arms, and a regal bearing. *Giselle*, *Swan Lake*, and *The Sleeping Beauty* called for sovereign demeanor and elegance of movement. Konstantin Sergeyev and Vladimir Preobrazhensky in the thirties and forties, and Vladilen Semenov and Yuri Soloviev in the sixties, were famous cavaliers.

Technique was not a factor in the roles Baryshnikov might perform, since his seemed, quite simply, to have no limits. With his pliant, elongated muscles and soft *plié*, he seemed well suited to a lyric-romantic *emploi*. On the other hand, his short stature, childlike face, with its wide expressive range, and his generally playful disposition seemed to indicate *demi-caractère* possibilities. But his body was too perfect a classically polished instrument to be limited to the *demi-caractère* repertoire (of which the buffoon in the Soviet version of *Swan Lake* is an example). It would have been like asking Maria Callas to sing nothing but Puccini operas.

Baryshnikov was difficult to categorize for another reason: he was exceptional. He stood out among the first-class dancers of the Kirov stage for his astonishing energy and bewitching speed of execution. According to Kirov old-timers, the legendary Vaslav Nijinsky had similar problems with *emploi*. For a romantic hero or *danseur noble* (and in the early 1900s the repertoire was exclusively romantic), he was somewhat stocky, his legs too short, his calves and thighs too developed. Many of his contemporaries, choreographers Fedor Lopukhov and Mikhail Fokine, for instance, felt that he was not a lyric-romantic dancer. The stories of Nijinsky's brilliance in *Giselle* may be part of the legend Diaghilev helped to create. Nijinsky's phenomenal technical gifts alone—his rare *ballon* and his beats—would have guaranteed his singularity. But it was his idiosyncratic, almost grotesque expressiveness that made him truly remarkable. Even for Anna Pavlova, usually hostile to "Diaghilev's pet," he remained unsurpassed as Petrouchka, as the slave in *Schéhérazade*, or as the Faun in *L'Après-midi d'un Faune*.

In his autobiography, *To Dance* (Knopf, 1978), Valery Panov points out Baryshnikov's "strangeness" as a dancer at the Kirov: "Even he was just different enough from the proper Kirov forms to have prompted derision when he first joined." Baryshnikov infused ordinary strings of steps with new vitality, which confused or even annoyed his colleagues at the Kirov. Some established soloists complained that they could hardly follow his darting around and others that Baryshnikov had nothing but a perfect technique.

It was, in fact, the perfection of his technique which constituted Baryshnikov's individuality at the outset of his career. Panov, Dolgushin, and Nureyev, on the other hand, gave classical roles a personal

◁ The Kirov rehearsal hall / N. SLEZINGER

interpretation, which compensated for their technical imperfections. In spite of his inadequate training, Nureyev immediately became a principal dancer, with the support of the leading ballerina of the Kirov, Natalia Dudinskaya, due to his strong and original performances in leading roles. Nureyev had not really absorbed the principles of the Russian school in the relatively short time—three years—he spent at the Vaganova School. Once in the West, he would switch, with characteristic eclecticism, to the English style.

But Misha flawlessly embodied the Russian principles. His training had endowed him with the absolute precision in the positioning of the head, arms, and legs distinctive of the Russian school. Baryshnikov's phenomenal technique has never been surpassed. His incredible grand pirouette recalled stories from the twenties of Vakhtang Chabukiani's legendary, seemingly effortless turns. And the abandon with which Baryshnikov executed double *tours* in the air and *rivoltades* reminded many Leningrad balletomanes of the young Alexei Yermolaev (current Bolshoi star Vladimir Vasiliev's former teacher). But from the beginning Baryshnikov's art displayed another distinctive trait—perfection that somewhat precluded emotional involvement.

Two types of dancer have been favored alternately throughout ballet history, one stressing virtuosity, the other emotional projection. One approach defined ballet's formal limits, while the other suggested means of transcending them. During the Romantic period (1830–50), virtuosity was secondary to a ballet's dreamy, poetic mood. Taglioni, sylph-like and innocent, embodied the Romantic image. In the second half of the nineteenth century, Marius Petipa went beyond the Romantic style by refining and expanding ballet technique. He created an elegant classicism best exemplified by his masterpiece, *The Sleeping Beauty* (1890).

In the early 1900s Mikhail Fokine reacted against Petipa's classicism by choreographing works in a neo-Romantic or neoclassical mode (*Les Sylphides, Petrouchka, Eunice*). A split occurred between those advocating technical bravura and those seeking to extend ballet's expressive possibilities. Fokine's dancers, including Pavlova, Nijinsky, Tamara Karsavina, and Olga Spessivtseva, belonged to the latter group, asserting their individuality as artists and dance's obligation to go beyond technique for technique's sake. Diaghilev's Saisons Russes (1909–29) nurtured this trend, out of which a new professionalism emerged. Technique became more than mere flourish; it was now an expressive medium in itself. These principles were later elaborated in the choreography of George Balanchine.

The split between the two schools of dancing was mended to an extent in the twenties, when Agrippina Vaganova, herself a virtuoso, fused them in her teaching technique. Both virtuosity and poetic expressiveness reestablished themselves on the Kirov stage in the pleiad of performers who had been her students: Marina Semenova, Natalia Dudinskaya, Galina Ulanova, and Alla Shelest. Though some of these stars left the Kirov in the thirties, their mode of performance continued to influence Kirov dancers throughout the sixties. But Baryshnikov, by virtue of his almost impersonally flawless style, stood apart from his predecessors.

Despite Baryshnikov's already extraordinary technique, few challenging roles were available to the young graduate at the beginning of his career. *The Sleeping Beauty*, *Giselle*, and *Swan Lake* were still considered out of the question. Misha was given roles which often fell short of fully exploiting his gifts.

For his debut with the Kirov company (1967), Baryshnikov danced the peasant pas de deux from *Giselle*'s first act. The Kirov production of this divertissement preserved Petipa's original choreography. (The American Ballet Theatre's *Giselle* makes use of a different version.) Baryshnikov executed his role's parade of beats and cabrioles as if they were child's play. Soon after, he performed the Blue Bird variation from *The Sleeping Beauty* and the romantic poet from Fokine's *Les Sylphides*. Both roles were among Yuri Soloviev's most perfect accomplishments, and in both Baryshnikov was miscast. Misha did not have Soloviev's unusual *ballon*—the capacity to "hang in the air"—which the Blue Bird needs.

Nor was *Les Sylphides'* romantic cavalier an ideal role for Baryshnikov. It demanded an air of meditative reticence and a mixture of detachment and mannered solicitude as a partner that did not really suit Misha. He successfully reproduced Fokine's style but his performance was merely correct. The ballet itself somehow suffered from the precision of Baryshnikov's execution, which highlighted its irremediably old-fashioned style.

Baryshnikov most often performed a concert program with a string of pas de deux (*Le Corsaire* or *Don Quixote*, for instance) that were threadbare even in Petipa's time. The paucity of the repertoire was aggravated by another problem—lack of an adequate partner. Misha danced with soubrette-like soloists, such as Olga Vtorushina or Svetlana Efremova, who were a far cry from the great ballerinas suitable to his talent. This problem of partnership was, in fact, never properly resolved at the Kirov: neither Alla Sizova, his first Giselle, nor the aging Ninel Kurgapkina, with whom he danced *Don Quixote*, nor Irina Kolpakova, his constant partner in later years, ever equaled him, though Kolpakova was the best among them.

Baryshnikov's physical appearance, his irresistible youthful charm, his confidence and buoyancy, all constituted something of a pitfall. He could all too easily be cast as a sterling lad, the one-dimensional character who appears in ballet after ballet, as the official image of Soviet youth, often a brave and vital cosmonaut or settler. Yuri Soloviev, for instance, with his pleasant, open, "country boy" face and powerful, muscular legs, was given the role of the Youth in Igor Belsky's *Leningrad Symphony* (a ballet about World War II and the Leningrad siege, set to Shostakovich's Seventh Symphony) and that of another, no less bland youth in Konstantin Sergeyev's *The Distant Planet*. Naturally, this kind of part also fell to Baryshnikov.

In 1968, Misha's "mini-première" in this capacity took place at a time when Oleg Vinogradov was trying to assert his choreographic influence—he and two others were to replace Sergeyev briefly in 1971. He offered Misha the role of the Youth in *The Mountain Girl*, which was set to Soviet composer Murad Kashlaiev's uninspired music and was based on a prose epic by Rasul Gamzatov, a prolific writer from the Caucasus.

In this work, the traditional ethics of the Caucasian mountain people are set against the salutary pragmatism of Soviet morality. Assiyat, the village beauty, is betrothed to the uncouth and passionate Osman, but Assiyat prefers Moscow University and the attentions of a young student—danced by Baryshnikov—who is just as eager to learn as she. This love costs Assiyat her life at the hands of the jealous Osman (performed by Valery Panov).

To make up for the ballet's insubstantiality, Vinogradov devised choreographic combinations as intricate as gymnastic stunts, relying on his dancers' exceptional skills. This "acrobatic" style would flourish in the seventies, since it filled out the otherwise flimsy structure of many ballets. And though the dancers far surpassed their material, athleticism at least made use of their strengths.

Vinogradov wisely gave Panov and Baryshnikov complete freedom. Rehearsals often resembled improvisations on a theme. Misha based his variations on the dizzying *rivoltades*, beats, double *tours en l'air*, and other breathtaking feats that were his forte since the Vaganova School.

The lighthearted barber Basil from Petipa's divertissement ballet *Don Quixote* was the only part in the classical Kirov repertoire that clearly fit Baryshnikov. He danced Basil during his second season at the Kirov (1968–69). This ballet was an example of Petipa's early grand classical style, which abounded in virtuoso passages but was overloaded with pantomime. Despite efforts to modernize it, *Don Quixote* tends to remain a venerable if essentially boring balletic monument. The ballet was preserved in both the Kirov and the Bolshoi repertoires due to the scarcity of Petipa works. Also, its combination

Exercising, flanked by Soloviev and Desnizky / N. SLEZINGER

of strict classical technique and style with a *caractère* (folkloric) flavor appealed to many generations of Russian dancers, some of whom revitalized it by approaching it in the spirit of farce or vaudeville.

Maya Plisetskaya and Vladimir Vasiliev, for example, infused life into the ballet's string of divertissements by following the guidelines of Konstantin Stanislavsky, who in his book, *My Life in Art*, championed realism in the theater: "When you act in vaudeville it is essential to believe in the primitive and even illogical situation." In Plisetskaya's and Vasiliev's interpretations, the disconnected interludes seemed to grow out of the characters' impulses and no longer appeared arbitrary. Plisetskaya's mischievously flirtatious Kitri was more than a music-hall character, though she resembled one with her gold hoops, the flower in her hair, and the curling ringlet on her forehead. Her Kitri had a vitality that turned the set into a real Spanish street, hot and dusty, the

sweet-smelling air filled with the sounds of merrymaking and heavy with passion.

Like Plisetskaya, Vasiliev shed a highly conventional mask, that of a rake and daredevil, for the traits of a living character. Coached by Alexei Yermolaev (who had performed Basil in the thirties), he danced with a pure zest that spoke for itself. The character came alive as Vasiliev saturated the variations in the final pas de deux with dazzling bravura tricks (such as double *sauts de basque*—the combination of jeté, then a grand *battement* through first position, and fouetté into attitude).

Baryshnikov made use of another approach, in which plot became a pretext for a stream of bravura dancing. Baryshnikov executed the movements with a mocking air, communicating an awareness of *Don Quixote*'s agreeable foolishness. His interpretation was in part justified by the utterly decrepit look of the Kirov production, which bore no resemblance to the sparkling production Baryshnikov later mounted at ABT. The costumes were drab and shabby; the scenery, a faded back-cloth, depicted a conventional sea of faded blue dotted with feebly drawn boats and sails. Such antediluvian bric-à-brac simply could not be taken seriously, even by an undemanding audience.

Moreover, Kitri was performed by Ninel Kurgapkina, who had coached Misha for the full-length production. One of the company's major soubrettes, Kurgapkina was by now almost forty and an unlikely object of Misha's juvenile ardor. Under the circumstances, Misha could not realistically portray Basil as a cunning rogue who manages to outsmart everybody in his zeal to marry Kitri—the traditional interpretation. Instead, Basil's pranks were performed for their own sake, and his mischief was playful, not scheming. As if the plot were incidental, Misha's carefree Basil detached itself from its absurdities. Even the virtuoso passages were performed with a kind of insouciance.

This unusual portrayal disconcerted even Baryshnikov's most fervent partisans. They attributed his iconoclasm to youth and to emotional immaturity, without realizing that the choice had been deliberate. Baryshnikov's intellectual approach to *Don Quixote*'s artificiality shed an ironic modern light on a well-worn classic. Nevertheless, he would later characterize it as the performance of an apprentice.

Despite the shortage of roles available to Baryshnikov during his first two seasons at the Kirov, an interesting opportunity did arise in the choreography of Igor Tchernichov. Tchernichov, whose successful career as a dancer had suddenly been interrupted by an injury, turned to choreography in 1967. After the favorable reception in Moscow of his first effort—an adagio set to the music of Albinoni—Igor set about composing a pas de deux to Berlioz's *Romeo and Juliet* for Natalia Makarova, his protégée, and the young Vadim Gulyayev. Vadim was a 1966 graduate of the Vaganova School and commanded distinctive lyrical and technical gifts.

When Misha joined the Kirov, Tchernichov decided to expand his original idea and create a one-act ballet. Misha would make an ideal Mercutio—his outlook on life coincided with the character's. Tchernichov first showed fragments of his *Romeo and Juliet* to friends and a few critics. All were enthusiastic, and all encouraged him to continue.

The ballet was rehearsed in fits and starts due to the tight schedules of all the participants. No thought was given to its eventual fate. But at the first official preview of the work in 1968, Sergeyev and Dudinskaya opposed it, and their word in effect determined the decision of the Art Committee, the Kirov's ultimate policy shapers. Tchernichov's unusual and daring choreography, with its unconventional lifts and turns, infuriated them for many reasons. It revealed the direct influence of Leonid Yakobson, the Kirov's only successful choreographic rebel, whose controversial style appalled them, and it recalled Roland Petit's *Notre-Dame de Paris*, which Sergeyev regarded as modernist trash. But, more important, the choreography was vulnerable because it was openly, if chastely, erotic. Eight years later, when Elena Tchernichova, Igor's ex-wife, resurrected this banned ballet in Baltimore, it no longer looked so daring. Its innovations paralleled those of choreographers like John Neumeier and Glen Tetley. But to a Soviet eye, this choreography blatantly overstepped the bounds of decorum. Eroticism threatened conventional morality, which it was Sergeyev's job to uphold.

Romeo and Juliet was banned on the spot, to the great distress of Natalia Makarova, who welcomed the chance to escape the routine of Romantic ballet by working in Tchernichov's neoclassical style. Later, she said the action taken against *Romeo and Juliet* was one of the causes of her defection.

But Tchernichov did not give up. He managed to get Irina Kolpakova interested in dancing the ballet (Makarova became unavailable, since she was constantly on tour abroad). Kolpakova was a Party member and wielded a certain influence in the upper echelons. Igor persuaded her to include *Romeo* on the program of a gala evening in which she was featured. The fact that Kolpakova presided over the anti-Sergeyev coalition at the Kirov played into Igor's hands, since she would not hesitate to sneak into the Kirov a ballet Sergeyev had once rejected.

Be that as it may, *Romeo* was ready to be performed by December 1969, with Gulyayev and Kolpakova cast as the lovers and Baryshnikov as Mercutio.

This *Romeo and Juliet* was conceived as a romantic drama of soaring, blind passion, of which Mercutio alone foresaw the consequences. The ballet had a choreographic audacity that had rarely been seen on the Kirov stage. The adagio abounded with eroticism in both *par terre* combinations and lifts: in its finale Juliet stepped with both feet onto Romeo's foot, and froze in a statue-like pose. The duel between Romeo and Tybalt was choreographed symbolically and performed without swords. (This trick, then new to Soviet ballet, was later used frequently by Sergeyev in his *Hamlet*, and then by Yuri Grigorovich in his less skillful version of *Romeo and Juliet*, set to Prokofiev's music and presented in New York in August 1979.)

When Tchernichov's *Romeo and Juliet* premièred on December 30, on the stage of the Industry House of Culture (the Kirov theater was undergoing repairs), Baryshnikov's Mercutio took the audience by storm. His rendition of the "Queen Mab" sequence, in particular, perfectly evoked the spirit of Mercutio's sardonic and frenzied speech. Baryshnikov began the solo with his back to the audience, flew without preparation into a double *tour*, and landed facing the audience in arabesque, dumbfounding it immediately with a string of swift *tours* and beats, performed at the highest speed. The impact was breathtaking. Irina Kolpakova, usually rather reserved, even frozen in her impeccability as Aurora or Giselle, suddenly thawed. For the first time, at thirty-six, she displayed warmth and lyricism.

But the ballet was performed only once: Kolpakova would not risk annoying the Party supervisors by further sponsoring the iconoclastic Tchernichov production. She put it away for better times and never returned to it.

Meanwhile, the collaboration between Baryshnikov and Tchernichov looked promising. In 1969 Igor was choreographing Ravel's *Bolero*, for both Misha and Yuri Soloviev. (Yuri planned to include *Bolero* in a solo production he was then preparing.) I watched Misha rehearse and witnessed what seemed almost like a contest between choreographer and dancer, each inspiring and spurring on the other's creativity. The choreography so suited Misha that it seemed spontaneous. Unfortunately, *Bolero* was also banned by Sergeyev.

Although Misha gave Sergeyev credit for his command of the classical heritage and for his ability to put together classical variations at a moment's notice, he strongly disapproved of the choreographer's conventional values. Sergeyev's unquestioning support of the official aesthetic code was unacceptable to Baryshnikov. Misha also found intolerable Sergeyev's habit of urging pious verities on others. Even now, Baryshnikov is not averse to mimicking his manner. He still vividly recalls a rehearsal at which Sergeyev was working with Nikita Dolgushin on the role of Prince Siegfried in *Swan Lake*. Because of a propensity for intellectualizing romantic parts, Nikita turned his hapless protagonist into a kind of melancholy Hamlet figure. His approach annoyed Sergeyev no end: the pessimistic key didn't correspond to the standards of Soviet optimism. "Why are you holding your bow and

With Peter Rachinsky and Ninel Kurgapkina / N. SLEZINGER

arrow as if gravitating toward the grave? Cheer up, head for the sun, for the sunshine illuminating your life."

But it was Sergeyev's hostility to Tchernichov which most thoroughly alienated Misha. As had been the case with Dolgushin, Sergeyev's motivation in opposing Tchernichov was, simply, jealousy. The roots of Sergeyev's dislike for Igor lay in his success as a dancer in ballets like *The Bronze Horseman* in which Sergeyev himself had once excelled. Igor's choreographic gift only compounded his envy.

Sergeyev realized that to permit new choreographic talent on the Kirov stage would jeopardize his own position. He justified his disapproval of Igor's first piece, a duet set to an Albinoni adagio, with a convenient ideological excuse—the work was not what the Soviet people needed. Further, he charged that Igor's ballet was infused with Western sentiments and incompatible with the "robust and life-affirming Soviet ballet." In his dispute with Sergeyev over the duet, Igor was recklessly outspoken, and in effect signed his own death warrant. As Elena Tchernichova told me, when Sergeyev inquired, in a tone of false innocence, as to the meaning of the piece, Tchernichov replied that it was about loneliness: "Human existence is a continual overcoming of loneliness. We are born alone and alone we die."

"What about love, then?"

"That's only a temporary salvation."

"And the collective? The Soviet collective, with its feeling of closeness, its solidarity? How can one speak of loneliness in our socialist society?"

Though Igor managed to stage the adagio for Alexander Godunov, then a member of a small classical troupe affiliated with the Moiseyev Ballet Company in Moscow, the work was banned from the Kirov stage.

3 STAR OF THE KIROV

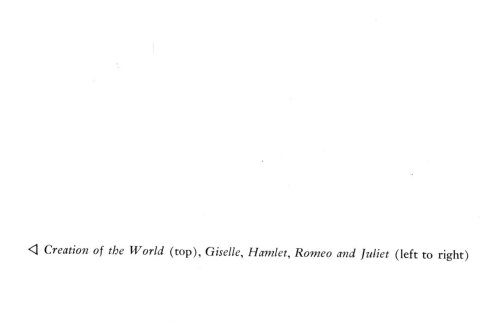

◁ *Creation of the World* (top), *Giselle, Hamlet, Romeo and Juliet* (left to right)

B Y HIS THIRD SEASON at the theater (1969–70), Baryshnikov was recognized as an absolute star, even by the highly demanding Leningrad audiences. Stardom in the Soviet Union doesn't entail fat fees or tremendous publicity; from 1967 to 1974 Baryshnikov gave only one newspaper interview, though his name was on everybody's lips.

The ballet star in Russia is, in fact, a *primus inter pares*—first among equals—favored only by a relatively high salary (at most 450 rubles a month, as opposed to 120 rubles a month for a member of the corps) and the recognition of the general public. Misha's first comfortable apartment was given to him not long before his defection (this apartment was not his own; it belonged to the state). Earlier, even after he had been made a Kirov principal dancer, he shared a room with another company member in a dormitory for young Kirov dancers. Then he lived with Kirov ballerina Tatiana Koltzova in a tiny, uncomfortable, one-bedroom apartment located on the Griboyedov Canal. (This arrangement lasted about a year.)

Though the material benefits of stardom were relatively modest, Baryshnikov, by virtue of his uniqueness, enjoyed certain artistic privileges. While he was still a young dancer, several original, if artistically uneven, roles had been created for him by the most talented Soviet choreographers. This happened quite rarely; Maya Plisetskaya, for example, was forty-two and an internationally famous ballerina before she danced a role created especially for her—Carmen in Alberto Alonso's production for the Bolshoi stage (1967). But at twenty-one Baryshnikov was already being favored by the attention of Leonid Yakobson.

In those days, Yakobson, known as the *enfant terrible* of Soviet ballet, was the most colorful figure at the Kirov. He was a product of the turbulent twenties and managed to preserve their rebellious spirit during the conformist fifties and sixties. Yakobson's choreography eludes easy definition. At times recalling Isadora Duncan's untrammeled fluidity or Fokine's neoclassic aestheticism, Yakobson's style freely combined pantomime, which verged on caricature, sculptural gesture, elements of pure classicism, and neoclassicism. He favored turned-in knees, as Fokine did (*les positions en dedans*), and consciously ungraceful poses, throwing the classically trained body slightly askew and substituting the unexpected for the familiar.

Yakobson was the Kirov's unconventional genius. With a kind of creative abandon, he sought to heighten ballet's expressiveness by combining various dance styles, like a lavish colorist mixing paints. Irrepressible and endowed with an inexhaustible imagination, Yakobson was now and then restrained by his superiors and his energy redirected into the proper channels. Reacting against official constraints, this imagination forsook moderation and propriety. His work united the excesses of bad taste with inspiration.

Yakobson created in an aesthetic vacuum, isolated from the work of Western choreographers like John Cranko, Jerome Robbins, and Martha Graham. Yet his work resembled theirs in that it, too, departed boldly from the classical tradition. Yakobson could be so uncompromising that he would flush with horror and indignation when a dancer warmed up for rehearsals with an arabesque or some *tours*. Still, he understood the classical vocabulary and used it to protect himself when attacked for "unaesthetic movements." "It only looks modern to you," he would say to his critics. "This jerking, as you permit yourself to describe it, is just a slightly altered *pas de bourrée*; what you call reeling, a typical *temps lié*."

Yakobson was both mocked and worshipped by the dancers themselves. His mischievous persistence in assigning them unaccustomed movements gave rise to a company ditty:

> The high point in their careers—
> the best in Europe
> forced to jump on their rears.

For *The Bedbug* (1965), which was based on Vladimir Mayakovsky's play, he dressed Makarova, an ideal Romantic ballerina who seemed to belong in a romantic tutu, in a short, tight 1920's skirt. Her Zoya Berezkina twitched in syncopated rhythm on high heels, wringing her hands at being deceived in love for the first time. He deliberately deprived Alla Osipenko, famous for her flowing, "singing" line, of any movement whatsoever in *Taglioni's Flight*. Her body, which seemed created for dancing, was instead carried about the stage by her partners, above whom she soared in a frozen arabesque, a symbol of immortal Romantic flight.

Baryshnikov, with his model academicism and exemplary purity of style, ought to have been unsuited to Yakobson's choreographic heresies. Performing in Yakobson's style might indeed have seemed a violation of Misha's identity as a dancer, were it not for Baryshnikov's protean nature. Clearly, there were strong affinities between the two men. Like Yakobson, Misha was irreverent. And his sense of theater was active both on stage and off, part of a mechanism to maintain the distance between self and world. This theatricality would be useful in Yakobson's *Vestris*.

Yakobson created *Vestris* for Baryshnikov to fulfill the requirements of an international ballet competition in Moscow (1969). The rules stated that Baryshnikov perform a work by a contemporary choreographer. Misha was nervous when he came over for dinner on the eve of his departure for Moscow. He had injured his foot and knew he would be competing against Hideo Fukagawa, a brilliant Japanese dancer. Under the circumstances, he felt he could hardly count on winning any prizes. Misha described *Vestris* as a typically Yakobsonian miniature, whose theme went beyond its title to embrace the whole of ballet history.

The work bore only a distant relationship to the legendary pair of Italian dancers who were active on the French stage in the late eighteenth and nineteenth centuries—Gaetan Vestris and his son, Auguste. The choreography never evoked Gaetan's model nobility or the image of Auguste soaring over the stage, only touching the ground, as his father affirmed, "out of regard for his comrades." Auguste was an innovator who introduced turns and leaps that were unusual for his time. But Yakobson's choreography emphasized *par terre* work, precluding such allusions. Nor did the ballet allude directly to Gaetan's independence of mind (he considered himself Voltaire's equal) or Auguste's amorous escapades.

Vestris's thematic vagueness met with disapproval in Leningrad, even among admirers of Yakobson's talent. The critics complained that Leonid Yakobson had his own notions of ballet history (erudition was, in fact, not Yakobson's strong point). But Moscow, responsive to any manifestation of seditious theatricality, reacted ecstatically. Yakobson had never intended to create a literal ballet. Though he and Baryshnikov studied old lithographs of the dancers and even consulted reference works, the Vestrises were only springboards for his fantasy. They appealed to him, of course, as convenient symbols of the free-thinking eighteenth century. But, more broadly, *Vestris* paid tribute to that century's great dance reformer and champion of the *ballet d'action*, Jean Georges Noverre, whose *Letters on the Dance* (1760) was a bible for the Frenchmen who laid Russian choreography's foundation, from Didelot to Petipa. In *Vestris* Yakobson implemented some of Noverre's key principles and displayed, almost emblematically, the "significant theatricality" that marked his style. For Yakobson, pure dance and pantomime should be used in conjunction with each other, as equally important elements. Their synthesis was what allowed a ballet to become fully expressive and successfully represent an idea. Baryshnikov, equally adept at pantomime and dance, was the ideal performer for *Vestris.*

Dressed in a waistcoat and tricot of gold color, Vestris-Baryshnikov appeared for the first time before the Moscow jury, which included Galina Ulanova, Alicia Alonso, Yuri Grigorovich, Maya Plisetskaya, and Vakhtang Chabukiani. Out of a possible twelve points, Plisetskaya, who became an instant fan of Baryshnikov's, gave him thirteen. "I was sitting there simply open-mouthed," she told me later, with her special candor. It wasn't only his extraordinary technique that she commented on; it was the phenomenal lightness with which he switched from a flurry of the most complex classical combinations to spectacular, grotesque pantomime. The parade of masks—the broken-down courtier, the brazen upstart, the arrogant nobleman—was fantastically theatrical, no matter whom he was portraying. "What difference does it make who the real Vestris was," Plisetskaya remarked, "now that I've seen the ballet theater of my dreams."

Baryshnikov won a gold medal for his performance. The medal was as much a tribute to his training in the Petersburg school as a recognition of his theatrical gifts. He had displayed such histrionic talent in *Vestris* that many felt Misha had a future as a dramatic dancer, and that Yakobson had mapped out the right path for his theatrical instincts. They may have been right, but circumstances oriented Baryshnikov in a different direction. He left to continue his ballet experiments in the West before having a chance to perform *Till Eulenspiegel,* or the ballet in the *commedia dell'arte* style that Yakobson was in the midst of preparing for him. Significantly, though, *Vestris* was the only neoclassical ballet Baryshnikov brought with him to the West; it was seen on American television as part of *Baryshnikov at Wolf Trap* in October 1976.

In a sense, Misha's obvious dramatic potential complicated his situation. The audience expected from him not only the technical wonders which they by now took for granted but also the strong dramatic impact without which ballet generally makes little sense to Russians.

stris première, 1969 / N. SLEZINGER

While Misha could amaze the British public during the Kirov's August 1970 tour in London (where critics unanimously pronounced him a genius), the spoiled Leningrad audience demanded that he go further, and, in a sense, surpass himself. But the Kirov repertoire presented Misha with no unusual challenges, and nothing promised to disturb the unruffled calm of this balletic swamp. In such a climate, Konstantin Sergeyev's long-nurtured *Hamlet* soon became the talk of the town. Sergeyev set about staging the work in early 1970, and there were those who had great hopes for this ballet, thinking it could provide Baryshnikov with a chance to display his dramatic powers.

Misha shared the role with Valery Panov and Yuri Soloviev, who dropped out very soon, calling the choreography "a series of classroom exercises set to phony music." Such harsh judgment seemed somewhat surprising, coming from Soloviev; he had a reputation for being phlegmatic and was a rather undemanding dancer, secretly preferring fishing to all balletic experimentation. Soloviev's opinion turned out to be justified, however.

Receiving the Moscow competition's gold medal from Galina Ulanova. Alicia Alonso (left and Konstantin Sergeyev (right) / N. SLEZINGER

Hamlet premièred on December 12, 1970. It was a typical drama ballet mounted in the best monumental tradition of Soviet kitsch. (Naturally, it won a state prize for the year's best ballet—further confirmation of its mediocrity, since fresh and original works never receive Soviet government prizes.)

Sergeyev did try to modernize the drama-ballet form with *Hamlet,* but his attempt was misguided. In an effort to outdo the Bolshoi's choreographic director, Yuri Grigorovich, who had declared war on balletic pantomime and staged his officially approved *Spartacus* in purely dance terms, Sergeyev had everybody dance in *Hamlet,* including the Ghost. Clad in a bluish gauze shroud, the Ghost emerged from the depths of the stage, doing a string of *tours chaînés* and gesticulating furiously. Sergeyev also had a childish notion that scissor-like leaps across the stage were enough to convey Hamlet's sworn commitment to revenge and that innumerable beats might express the essence of "To be or not to be." (No wonder that, after *Hamlet*'s preview, this monologue was sneered at as "To beat or not to beat . . .")

Sergeyev's choreography was a perfect example of pure formalism, based on the bizarre assumption that just the steps themselves, regardless of their arrangement, are enough to express emotion and dramatic consistency. *Hamlet* exemplified this new trend in Soviet ballet, which Arlene Croce spotted in Grigorovich's "everyone-must-dance" version of *Romeo and Juliet,* performed in August 1979 by the Bolshoi during its New York "Mass Defection Season":

> The tendency of Russian ballet in the twenty years since its reintroduction to the West has been toward a simulation of pure expression—not dance as metaphor but dance as not mime, a definition arrived at by negation and without further qualification. This, of course, creates a literalism that can be subjected to simple empirical tests and an emptiness that can be filled by intellectual apologetics.

The straightforwardly illustrative function of the scenery reinforced this literalism. Since Shakespeare compared Denmark to a dungeon, each of designer Sofia Yunovich's eleven alternating backcloths depicted Elsinore's stone walls, high, dismal turrets, and barred windows. The castle interior, an ellipse-like construction shaped like a mini-hippodrome, occupied the whole stage. Sergeyev used the set awkwardly: at one point, Hamlet-Baryshnikov—wearing white tights,

London, 1970: (opposite page, left to right) Osipenko, Sizova, Baryshnikov, Makarova, Soloviev; and on trampoline, Crystal Palace Sports Ground; (below, right to left) Sergeyev, Baryshnikov, Dudinskaya, Kolpakova, Rachinsky / ROSEMARY WINCKLEY

In London, 1970 / ROSEMARY WINCKLEY

a black velvet waistcoat, and a gold medallion with his father's picture—ran down the semicircular stage to "stumble" onto his mother, Gertrude, clinging in passionate embrace to his Uncle Claudius.

In a vain attempt at originality, and as if to compensate for his lack of choreographic ideas, Sergeyev departed from Shakespeare by opening the ballet with the funeral of Hamlet's father. Gertrude and Claudius, attended by mourners and a throng of subjects, strolled in solemn procession, simulating grief. (Fortunately, Sergeyev did not go as far as starting the ballet with Hamlet's pre-Wittenberg childhood, as Vakhtang Chabukiani had done in his five-act Georgian production in Tbilisi in 1974.) Sergeyev's highly literal use of props was enough to subvert his claim to inventiveness. Ophelia enshrouded herself in a blue scarf to signify she was drowning, while Claudius and Gertrude shared a gigantic blood-red nuptial bed bespeaking lust and crime. In full accordance with Soviet optimism, which had already made sure Odette survived in *Swan Lake*'s finale, Hamlet seemed to remain alive at the end; at any rate, he froze in an ecstatic, falsely significant pose, his eyes fixed on the sky, presumably still looking for the answer to the questions that had tormented him.

This agglomeration of absurd clichés insulted Misha's aesthetic feelings. The role made excellent use of his physical abilities, but could not fire his imagination. It provoked instead a mixture of embarrassment and resentment he could barely conceal even while performing. After the preview he asked me if I'd found the production even slightly bearable—a question that unfortunately anticipated my less than encouraging reply.

Nevertheless, *Hamlet* was pronounced a new achievement in Soviet art by the official reviewers; any criticism of it, including my review for the newspaper *Smena*, could not be published because the press was controlled entirely by Sergeyev's influential patrons from the Party's Central Committee. However, many of the Kirov's principal dancers privately referred to the ballet as a "choreographic void" and a "sorry farce." Following Yuri Soloviev's example, Misha dropped out after two performances, saying that he could not dance a *Hamlet* devoid of consistency. Only Valery Panov, who had alternated with Baryshnikov in the role, still waxed enthusiastic over Sergeyev's creation, though many agreed with ballet historian Natalia Roslavleva's review, which judged that "the pure classical dictionary on which Hamlet's part is based was simply beyond the range of an excellent *demi-carac-*

tère dancer like Panov." Panov felt Misha's withdrawal was detrimental to his artistic development, and in his autobiography, *To Dance*, suggests that Misha "became trapped in the web woven by the anti-Sergeyev spiders." But Baryshnikov refused the role because his aesthetics had grown incompatible with Sergeyev's approach.

Another disappointment followed with *The Prince of the Pagodas*, a ballet set, promisingly, to Benjamin Britten's music and staged by Oleg Vinogradov. The production turned out to be a purely formalistic *tour de force*, with a fairy-tale plot. Characteristically, Vinogradov gave Baryshnikov a series of acrobatic tricks and intricate combinations devoid of dramatic consistency. The result was yet another unfulfilling part at a time when no others seemed likely to emerge.

However, a role soon appeared from an unexpected quarter. One of Leningrad's most gifted leading actors, Sergei Yursky, offered Baryshnikov the role of the toreador in his television dramatization of Hemingway's *The Sun Also Rises* (1971). Baryshnikov accepted, prompting a storm of arguments in Leningrad's theatrical circles. There were protests that dancers rarely display acting talent in non-dancing screen roles. That objection carries a certain amount of truth. Even a great tragedienne like Maya Plisetskaya was unconvincing as the Princess Betsy Tverskaya in the movie *Anna Karenina*. And dancers are often self-conscious about their unnaturally turned-out gait or their exaggeratedly broad carriage. Yursky's idea may have seemed somewhat Utopian, but he overruled his colleagues' arguments. Misha had a quality Yursky was looking for—Baryshnikov would simply be himself on a television screen.

Yursky's intuition did not deceive him. Misha was a sensation. He seemed utterly natural in front of the camera. To a modest speaking role he brought an eloquent non-verbal dimension. His dance training gave a special compressed energy to his glances, movements, and gestures, and his performance far surpassed the others', though all but him were professional actors.

Soon after his triumph, choreographer Kirill Laskari cast Misha in a made-for-television ballet, *The Tale of Serf Nikishka* (a variation of the Firebird fairy tale). This television production, though it boasted Misha's near-perfect partnership with Alla Osipenko as the Firebird, did not show Baryshnikov to best advantage. Misha's peasant garb looked artificial, and the camera caught and emphasized every theatrical contrivance. The work was out of place on television, and Baryshnikov out of place in it. Live performance remained a better medium.

That same year, 1971, he returned to his element, performing in a new ballet, *The Creation of the World*. Moscow's gifted ballet masters Natalia Kasatkina and Vladimir Vasiliev had been invited to stage a Bolshoi production on the Kirov stage, and they chose *Creation*. The ballet was based on French caricaturist Jean Effel's unremarkable series of biblical satires and was choreographed to Andrei Petrov's equally unremarkable music. But out of these elements came an unusually sophisticated, lively work.

The Bolshoi's theatrical flair often led to genuine innovation, at least since Alexander Gorsky's reforms in the first two decades of this century. Here, Fokine's Sylphides and Ivanov's swans vanished, and a series of caricatures appeared on the old imperial stage. Yuri Soloviev played God, dressed in a traditional peasant's tunic, rather like a nightshirt. His accompanying host of angels and archangels in long, dignified robes looked just as Russian. (Apparently, the designer, Enar Stenberg, assumed that the world had been created on the Russian steppes.) Valery Panov was the Devil, who had dragged himself out of hell by the tail, joined by a female companion—a she-devil temptress (Kaleria Fedicheva or Galina Panova). Her objective was to seduce the newly created Adam—Baryshnikov—but the charms of Irina Kolpakova as Eve prevailed. Today, many in Leningrad recall this production nostalgically, since most of its original cast will never return to the Kirov stage. Yuri Soloviev—God—committed suicide in the winter of 1977. The Panovs, Devil and she-devil, left Russia in 1974 after being harassed for twenty-seven months by the KGB. The summer of that same year, Baryshnikov requested political asylum in Canada. In February 1975, Kaleria Fedicheva left to join her husband in the United States. Only Kolpakova remained behind as a relic of the ballet's past glory.

The set for *The Creation of the World* represented the biblical hierarchy by means of a construction depicting heaven, earth, and hell. God swooped in with his angels, who appeared on a stage framed with gigantic oxeye daisies (a Russian folk symbol for chastity), in trees and in clouds made of lace appliqués. Just in case the ballet seemed too light or ideologically insubstantial, the choreographers paid homage to the principles of socialist realism. They superimposed ideological trappings on pure entertainment to avoid official censure. As a result, the proceedings arbitrarily included an atomic explosion, after which humanity was resurrected. And the ballet's finale also appeared to be a kind of insurance. In it, the progeny of Adam and Eve, who had been driven from the Garden of Eden to be fruitful and multiply, galloped madly about the stage against a backdrop depicting the Sistine Chapel frescoes, to the final movement of Beethoven's Ninth Symphony. This ending guaranteed the moral seriousness of an otherwise unorthodox ballet. Indeed, *The Creation of the World* was, by the usual Soviet standards, astoundingly entertaining and irreverent.

First of all, its God creates the world out of boredom. Yuri Soloviev, displaying hitherto hidden comic gifts, had been pining away in paradise. Heaven was illuminated from upstage by a single star shining dully on its wooden support. Soloviev, looking like a zealous Russian muzhik with his long, white shirt, beard, light-brown hair, and round, trusting face, kept busy by inspecting his thoroughly ordinary household or flying up into the clouds over the angels' heads. (The latter kept up a continuous flutter of wings.) Or God could survey the non-activity of his two negligent archangels. In fact, there was not much to do in paradise and God might have died of boredom were it not for the appearance of the charmingly boastful and self-assured Devil, Valery Panov, who was also languishing. To break the routine, the Devil extinguishes the star and plunges the stage into darkness, then engages God in a childishly innocent game of blindman's bluff. The sequence featured the dizzying leaps and jetés at which the two dancers were masters.

As in Bulgakov's *The Master and Margarita*—the ballet may have been a takeoff on the novel—the Devil was here an instigator of good deeds. Had God and the Devil not bumped heads and accidentally ignited the sun, creative inspiration might never have seized the bearded old gentleman. As it was, tired of sitting still among the daisies in a now-sunny paradise, God decided to take up sculpture. He began diligently kneading clay on a hillock upstage, managing to fashion a lump of sorts. Disappointed and on the point of giving up, he waved a dismissive arm at the shape, and it suddenly sprang to his feet.

The creation turned out to be as silly as it was comely, a pretty baby with sawdust between its ears instead of a brain. Baryshnikov mimed Adam to perfection. Comedy—a rare treat at the prim and proper Kirov—was very much Baryshnikov's element. It was difficult not to be touched by the childish concentration with which he observed his own feet and pulled them toward his mouth, took his first

Creation of the World, (right) with Irina Kolpakova / N. SLEZINGER

unsteady steps, raced about excitedly with the little angels, and sat down to make mud pies. Baryshnikov's Adam was a big child gradually growing out of his baby fat, eager to be independent of his progenitor and guardian angels, who were simply not very interesting playmates anymore. That moment of independence neared when, fully coordinated at last, Baryshnikov's Adam began to dance. The Kirov stage had perhaps not seen such virtuosity since Nijinsky's time. The choreographers indeed seemed to be testing virtuosity's limits in Misha's combinations. In the last act, for instance, Adam-Baryshnikov, seized by a frenzy of love for Eve, executed a series of *rivoltades*, but without

Creation of the World, curtain call with Irina Kolpakova, Kirov theater / N. SLEZINGER

landing in the ordinary fashion; he shifted in the air and began yet another set.

The understanding that went into Misha's performance deepened the emotional tenor of the production. His Adam changed over the course of the ballet, growing from child to adult. As the character matured, the work took on a new, lyrical quality. Newborn Adam's curiosity (quite a contrast to God's boredom) was the kind that killed the cat. God barely saved him from literally falling for the Devil's ruses and plummeting to the netherworld. When the cunning Devil tempts Adam with his she-devil, God creates Eve from Adam's rib to protect him from still another danger.

Irina Kolpakova's Eve matched Adam-Baryshnikov perfectly. Like Juliet in the Tchernichov ballet, this was a role in which Kolpakova went beyond flawless pointwork and exemplary *port de bras*. Her customary coldness disappeared in an abundance of genuine lyricism. In a twiglike fashion she clutched God's hand, then somnolently opened her arms like the petals of a flower. On awakening, she proved as curious as Adam. Awed contemplation of the unknown creature was not enough to satisfy her, and she darted impatiently toward him. Adam and Eve made friends by crawling toward each other like two awkward puppies, until they froze in genuine bewilderment, and Eve, taking courage, put her finger in Adam's astonished mouth. Then came a playful dance competition, with each one attempting to outdo the other.

After this rite of acquaintance and awakening love, Adam-Baryshnikov suddenly shed his charming nonchalance, revealing an unexpected vulnerability. For the first time, Baryshnikov let lyricism and tenderness filter out from behind the ironic mask.

From this point on, Adam and Eve's love determined the action, making their expulsion from Eden inevitable—the apple seemed only an incidental factor. Their attraction had to propel them into human destiny and adult responsibility.

But it was Baryshnikov's presence as an actor, more than his technical virtuosity, that distinguished his performance. His dynamism infused the ballet with vitality. He stood out among the cast, centering the work on himself, as Plisetskaya or Vasiliev had done in *Don Quixote*. In *The Creation of the World*, Baryshnikov, at twenty-three, laid claim to artistic maturity. Dancer and actor had fully merged for the first time. Confirming this, the ballet historian and critic Vera

Krassovskaya, in her review for *Teater* magazine, noted that *The Creation of the World* marked the end of Baryshnikov's apprenticeship. Everything that had happened earlier was "before Adam."

With *The Creation of the World*, Misha won the recognition of those who had revered him as a virtuoso but still underestimated him as an actor. Now he had to prove to the Kirov management and to skeptics that he was able to master *Giselle* and *Swan Lake*. *The Sleeping Beauty*, which he danced frequently, did not present any challenge; the ballet was a showcase for its Auroras and Lilac Fairies, but Prince Desiré, as he was called in the Kirov version, did no real dancing until the final act.

By contrast, *Giselle*'s Albrecht was one of the great classical male roles. During the sixties Kirov dancers were divided in their approach to the role. One school of interpretation had its ideological roots in the twenties and thirties, when *Giselle*, a Romantic ballet, had been presented as a drama of social inequality. This approach shared the prevailing Soviet aesthetic, which held that even Wagner's *Der Ring des Nibelungen* exemplified the class struggle. In this light, *Giselle* became the story of a naïve peasant girl betrayed by an immoral, callous Count Albrecht. None of the period's great Albrechts (Konstantin Sergeyev and Vakhtang Chabukiani at the Kirov and Alexei Yermolaev at the Bolshoi), though their characterizations were distinct, exceeded the social confines of the part. All of them portrayed Albrecht's contrition as the repentance of a rake. Sergeyev's interpretation was the most romantic of the three and therefore the most traditional, closest to the canon established by Pavel Gerdt, Pavlova's teacher. Sergeyev's approach influenced those of Yuri Soloviev, Sergei Vikulov, and Vladilen Semenov in the 1960s. Their Albrechts seemed more like static Romantic masks than living characters. Chabukiani, less conventional than Sergeyev in the role, infused the faithless count with his own Georgian impetuosity and dynamism. Yermolaev portrayed Albrecht as a blasé cad, ennobled by a belated repentance which revived his dormant humanity.

By the end of the 1950s, another approach to the role emerged among the Makarova-Nureyev generation. In the warmth of Khrushchev's liberal thaw, outstanding Soviet dancers such as Nikita Dolgushin and Rudolf Nureyev at the Kirov and Vladimir Vasiliev at the Bolshoi began to interpret *Giselle* as a kind of psychological drama. They rejected the threadbare idea of Albrecht as a merciless aristocrat whose character was derived from his social position. Their attitude was to an extent a rebellion against the Marxist determinism that had held the Soviet arts in an iron grip.

Dolgushin portrayed Albrecht as a Hamlet figure, a tormented intellectual for whom the simplehearted peasant girl Giselle embodied the Rousseau-like ideal of a natural, uncorrupted, guileless being. His love for Giselle was more intellectual curiosity than passion. And in Act II, he was not so much concerned with escaping the vindictive Wilis as enchanted by the mysterious appearance of his dead love and blissful at their reunion beyond the grave. Less restrained, Nureyev approached *Giselle* as a drama of passion. He infused the role of the romantic count with Tartar ebullience, even to excess. His flamboyance was out of keeping with the ballet's Romantic reticence and detrimental to its style. This passion, though, recalled Chabukiani's earlier fervor in the role.

Vasiliev took the psychological dimension even further. Alexei Yermolaev coached him in the role, and like Yermolaev, Vasiliev's Albrecht was transformed by Giselle's fate. In this case, Albrecht was more than just repentant; Giselle's death, a result of his juvenile irresponsibility, forced him to reassess his attitudes. Vasiliev's Albrecht was a young man awakening slowly to maturity through an agonizing process of self-examination.

Against this background, Baryshnikov's Albrecht looked more than iconoclastic. At his debut performance in 1972, Alla Sizova danced Giselle. Sizova was well known for her performance in *The Sleeping Beauty* in the early sixties as a frail, radiant Aurora. In 1972, however, only a hint of her former exuberance remained. She possessed a big natural jump but lacked the natural *plié* that usually mitigates the landing, and as a result developed a serious back injury. It undermined her confidence; she began to fear jumping, and at times looked shaky onstage. Sizova had never excelled at dramatic projection, and even in her prime, her Giselle was not memorable. Only her steady partnership with Misha during many performances of *Don Quixote* and *The Sleeping Beauty* justified her as a choice in this case. But the contrast between the dancers' approaches generated a curiously jarring effect and intrigued the audience. Sizova performed her Giselle as a balletic task, in the impersonal key adopted by Dudinskaya or Kolpakova. In contrast with Sizova's uninspired academicism, Baryshnikov's Albrecht seemed especially striking. Although he had been coached by Vladilen

Semenov, who epitomized the old-fashioned Kirov style, his interpretation was anything but traditional.

In his book, *Baryshnikov at Work*, Misha writes that he chose Albrecht's sincere love for Giselle as his key to the part. He thought of Albrecht as unwilling to endanger this genuine emotion, a first love, by revealing his true identity. Misha's interpretation was based on numerous performances and years of refinement, but the core of his approach had been visible from the first. Baryshnikov's innovations were triggered by the challenge of convincing the Kirov that he was dancer and actor enough to perform a part which many colleagues thought beyond his range.

Misha's eager boyishness was that of a young romantic poet who only happened to be a count. Youthfully enthusiastic, unreflective, this Albrecht stood at the other end of the spectrum from Dolgushin's anguished visionary. (Misha had seen his slightly overintellectualized 1968 performance opposite Natalia Makarova.) For Misha's Albrecht, Giselle is a first love, an ideal dreamed of in youthful reveries. He never intends to deceive her. An irresponsible, inexperienced youth, he delights in his emotions and in winning the timid Giselle's trust. The success of his suit fills him with happiness, and he gives no thought to the consequences, to the problems their class difference would create. Indeed, his love for a peasant girl is an escape from social convention and prejudice.

Act I of *Giselle*, in which Albrecht dances very little, allowed Baryshnikov to show his skill as an actor. Chaste love, not passion, drove his Albrecht; he played even the scene of his unmasking with touching naïveté, as if to say: "Yes, I am a count and betrothed to another woman. But this betrothal has nothing to do with love. It's you I love, and that's what counts . . ." And when the grieved Giselle dies, Baryshnikov's Albrecht is simply stunned, not repentant. Tragedy has occurred unexpectedly. He loves the girl, but circumstances have destroyed everything at once—a human life, his hopes and dreams. Contrary to Kirov tradition, Albrecht did not run offstage. He remained motionless, faced with the numbing irrationality of death.

Act II was even less conventional. Since her death, Giselle has become Albrecht's unattainable ideal, a romantic dream. It is not out of guilt that he now approaches her grave but to evoke her image in his memory. In the quiet, moonlit cemetery, he gives free rein to poetic reverie. The Wilis and Giselle herself thus materialize as the visionary creations of a fevered imagination.

The first appearance of Giselle's ghost seems a momentary hallucination. Ethereal, a pure, white essence, she brushes him with a flower and vanishes so fast he catches only empty air. When she reappears, Albrecht frowns, puzzled and intrigued. Is this real? Then he does a high *jeté entrelacé*, as if to signal his desire to get hold of Giselle and become one with her. His passion is that of a poet who has chanced upon his dream.

Baryshnikov's approach was unique in its sensitivity to the Romantic symbolism at work in Act II. The Wilis, dancing spirits of German mythology, are the ghosts of chaste brides who died on the eve of their wedding day. In Théophile Gautier's libretto for *Giselle*, these brides turn into Wilis only if they loved dancing more than anything else in life. Giselle's mother is convinced that if her "crazy daughter died, she would become a Wili and continue dancing after death." The Wilis' dancing, on the level of the plot, is a means of punishing male intruders. But on another, symbolic level, their dancing is what allows the Wilis to exist beyond the grave. The Wilis' graveyard is a privileged, transcendent realm, a world beyond both life and death. By mercilessly forcing each intruder to dance until he drops, the Wilis test his ability to enter their world and to endure its challenge. Giselle's other suitor, the gamekeeper Hilarion, fails the test and perishes. Though his love for Giselle is meant to be as strong as Albrecht's, it is worldly love, inconsonant with Romantic values.

As a sensitive dreamer, Baryshnikov's Albrecht is by contrast better suited to live through this marathon. In his initial duet with Giselle, he demonstrates his allegiance to his dead love and, by extension, to her new entourage. Now, in Act II's decisive variation, he has to prove his right to penetrate the Wilis' world. Dancers usually underscored Albrecht's desire merely to survive his ordeal, but from the start, Baryshnikov infused his variation with new vitality and determination, beginning with three sequences of steps moving diagonally across the stage (glissade, cabriole, coupé, *assemblé, entrechat six*).

Usually, the combination flowed smoothly, forming an uninterrupted wavy line. Baryshnikov broke that evenness deliberately by violently pushing off the stage into abrupt jumps and by executing the beats with unusual vehemence. His cabrioles looked especially daring.

In the academically correct position the torso leans in at a 45-degree angle, but Baryshnikov threw himself back 60 degrees. This tour de force imparted new meaning to the familiar string of steps, and Albrecht's first response to the Wilis' challenge took on new energy.

The second part of the variation includes *tours en l'air*, pirouettes, and chassés. The sequence is meant to express Albrecht's exhaustion. Contrary to tradition, Baryshnikov executed steps vigorously and at great momentum—his *tours* led directly into swift *renversés*. Albrecht's two diagonal sets of fast *brisés*, in which he pleads for the Queen of the Wilis' mercy, were performed at greater than usual speed. Vis-à-vis the severe Myrtha, he was intransigent even in supplication.

Baryshnikov was also innovative in his use of flowers as symbols in *Giselle*. Gautier's libretto confirms their emblematic role: "In the bright sunshine of the morning, the Wilis seem to droop and diffuse. One after another, they fade among the bushes and flowers from which they had emerged in the beginning. Thus, at daybreak, the night flowers wither." (In Perrot-Petipa's original version, Giselle disappears not into the grave but skyward, wreathed in flowers; for some reason, this symbolic detail was lost in the Kirov and American Ballet Theatre productions.)

Without looking up the Gautier text, Baryshnikov sensed the function of the flowers. In *Baryshnikov at Work* he outlines it: "The flowers are crucial . . . They are a symbol of his [Albrecht's] pain and they are a symbol of Giselle, too. Giselle expresses herself through flowers when she dances with the lilies, throwing them to him as if to say, 'Yes, these flowers are a part of me. They are me. I know you must have them.' And then later Giselle again uses the flowers to appease Myrtha . . . Here it's as if she says, 'See how strong my bond with this man is. Take these flowers and know it.'" And by strewing flowers in a straight line from the grave, Baryshnikov's Albrecht tries "to save [Giselle] for himself, to hold on to the final link between them." Though Giselle slips away, the flowers embody her presence in the natural world, reminders of an indestructible love.

Baryshnikov's unusual approach to Albrecht was especially well highlighted by his partnership with Bolshoi star Natalia Bessmertnova, who made numerous guest appearances at the Kirov. Along with Natalia Makarova, she had been regarded as one of the two perfect Giselles in Russia since her debut in 1962. If Makarova's unworldly heroine

evoked the image of Ulanova's simple, lighthearted peasant girl, Bessmertnova's Giselle reminded old-timers of the legendary Olga Spessivtseva, whom Russian ballet critic Akim Volynsky called "the
weeping spirit."

Frail, with Oriental features, and recalling Olga Spessivtseva's long
arms that bent strikingly at the wrists, Bessmertnova on stage evoked
the image of a frightened bird. Her Giselle was strange, otherworldly
from the outset—a mysterious, tragic figure who seemed to contain a
kind of doom. Such a Giselle might fire the romantic imagination of
Baryshnikov's Albrecht, and indirectly, Bessmertnova reinforced the
psychological motivation of his behavior; their partnership lent additional consistency to the drama.

She was an ideal partner for Baryshnikov. Along with the Kirov's
stagnant repertoire, this relationship may have prompted him to consider joining the Bolshoi. In 1972 Misha even began talking with the
Bolshoi's choreographic director, Yuri Grigorovich, but nothing ever
materialized. In truth, Grigorovich was not interested in having Baryshnikov at the Bolshoi. As a dancer, Misha was too refined for the
monumental ballets in the socialist-realist tradition, like *Spartacus* or
Ivan the Terrible, which he was then planning. Also, Baryshnikov's
appearance might have caused some problems with Mikhail Lavrovsky,
Bessmertnova's usual partner. Or it could have provoked a conflict
with Vladimir Vasiliev, the Bolshoi's leading male star, whose talent
contributed greatly to the success of Grigorovich's ballets in Moscow.
And although Vasiliev in one of his interviews called Baryshnikov "the
greatest classical dancer in the world," it seemed more reasonable for
both to enjoy their status in different companies.

That Misha's Bolshoi dreams never came true was by no means to
his detriment. Aside from his *Nutcracker* (1966), Grigorovich would
not have been able to offer him anything new. And Misha could perform *Legend of Love* (Grigorovich's most interesting ballet, created in
1961) or the old *Swan Lake* (from which Grigorovich's Bolshoi version differed only slightly) in his Leningrad alma mater.

It is not well understood in the West how difficult it is for a major
dancer, especially one of Baryshnikov's caliber, to be tied to the stage
of the Kirov or the Bolshoi, like a serf to his master's estate. He is not
allowed to go on tour abroad as a guest artist with other companies;
and he does not want to go on tour inside the Soviet Union. The
provincial theaters are like artistic graves. Party censorship is more

effective locally, since regional officials are careful to obey Moscow's instructions to the letter. Worse, the dancers suffer from the usual provincial scarcity of food, clothes, and other necessities. Therefore, in order not to lose the privilege of performing on the Kirov or the Bolshoi stage, a major dancer must withstand the onslaught of competitors, who will often employ Machiavellian means against him, including political denunciation and accusations of sexual deviance or moral depravity. As the Bolshoi Opera star Galina Vishnevskaya-Rostropovich once said to me: "The Kirov or the Bolshoi is akin to a huge bottle, stopped up with artists, and everybody is a cork to the other. All of them are tied to the same stale repertory and the same stage, and there is no exit, as in the hell of Sartre's famous play."

Misha's unsuccessful attempt to leave the Kirov may have made him more aware of his own "no exit" situation. After mastering *Giselle*, he had reached an artistic dead end.

His triumph in *Giselle* had another, positive consequence: for the first time since Nijinsky, he put to shame the Kirov's revered notion of balletic *emploi*. He proved that a dancer of his caliber could master any ballet style.

4 FOREBODINGS

◁ On the Nevsky Prospekt / N. SLEZINGER

THE SCANDAL that erupted over the defection of Natalia Makarova in the autumn of 1970 hit the Leningrad KGB like a bombshell. After failing to prevent Rudolf Nureyev's departure in 1961, the Kirov had again transgressed—a sure sign that ideological control over the theater was not sufficiently strong and that the in-house informers had been slipshod. But it was the unforgivably negligent KGB which suffered the harshest reprisals. Many members were demoted, removed from office altogether, or deprived of extra benefits like big salaries and access to scarce goods. It turned out they had been following Baryshnikov around instead of Makarova. A photograph of Misha walking down a London street with four goons tailing him showed up somehow in Leningrad and made the rounds of ballet circles. The KGB were not alone in paying for their incompetence; they were obliged to share the blame with someone in the Kirov hierarchy. Peter Rachinsky, thanks to his powerful ties with the Leningrad Regional Party Committee, came through the scandal caused by the "betrayer of the homeland, Makarova," unscathed. (Later he too would fall, accused of diverting funds from a department of Intourist and sharing the money with comrades "higher up"—an oblique explanation for his escaping blame in the so-called Makarova case.)

The rule of guilt by association operative at all levels of Soviet society required that a scapegoat be found who would have no friends on high. By an ironic twist of fate, this victim turned out to be Konstantin Sergeyev. In the early seventies, Sergeyev was deprived of his supporters in the Central Committee (notably, Frol Kozlov), who lost their positions as a result of Nikita Khrushchev's dismissal. Knowing this, Irina Kolpakova entered the fray with an army of supporters. For years, she had nurtured the thought of driving Sergeyev out of the Kirov and putting her husband, Vladilen Semenov, in his place. Sergeyev was vulnerable on all sides, and his days as chief choreographer at the Kirov theater were numbered.

His wife, Natalia Dudinskaya, also came under attack. An experienced teacher, she had perfected Makarova's fouetté and *renversé*, which at that time were the ballerina's weak points, but had neglected to instruct her ward in the spirit of Communist morality. As punishment, her advanced classes were simply taken away, leaving her with only her lessons at the Vaganova School. Moreover, Sergeyev, at work on *Hamlet*, was deprived of an experienced coach.

Life in the Soviet Union may be likened to treading on a rotten floor that may collapse at any moment. You fall through and never get out of the cellar again. You are ostracized, if discreetly, and helpless against those in authority. The formerly all-powerful Sergeyev found himself in just such a position. Everything that the Party supervisors had previously ignored now came down on Sergeyev's head: his misuse of power, his favoritism, his gay inclinations (which he had tried to conceal), the religious beliefs that prevented him from becoming a Party member, and his collection of icons. He and Dudinskaya were called to task for illegally selling foreign goods, which they brought back in great quantities from trips abroad. Even a scandal involving diamonds stolen from Dudinskaya in a London hotel was dragged in. She had demanded as compensation a sum far greater than the gems' declared value.

Furthermore, Sergeyev was blamed for the Kirov's musty repertoire, and for its general deterioration. By 1970, during its London summer season, the Kirov performed no complete ballets except *Giselle* and a few concert pieces. As always, the company got by on the strength of its stars—Osipenko, Soloviev, Makarova, and the still quite young Baryshnikov. But the repertoire really did look dull in comparison with the Bolshoi's, especially since Yuri Grigorovich (thrown out of the Kirov by Sergeyev) had taken charge. In six years' time, Grigorovich had created a new version of *The Sleeping Beauty* (1965); a new *Nutcracker* (1966), with a marvelous first act; and *Spartacus* (1968), in which Vladimir Vasiliev shone yet again. Grigorovich was also working on a new production of *Swan Lake*. (The last project came to naught, however, since it ended with the deaths of Odette and Siegfried—in keeping with Tchaikovsky's music —and was deemed too pessimistic. The Minister of Culture, Ekaterina Furtseva, nipped the work in the bud.)

Sergeyev had held his own for many years merely by mending classical masterpieces, but he knew that his hour had come and did not put up much of a fight.

In his autobiography, Valery Panov complains that "a bloodthirsty viciousness had been injected into the anti-Sergeyev campaign. Ballet's noblest Prince was dragged to Party sessions and vilified at meetings of a dozen Kirov committees." Even as a gesture of thanks to Sergeyev, who used Panov in nightmarish ballets such as *The Distant Planet* and *Hamlet*, this sounds like hyperbole. Panov seems not to take into account the talents Sergeyev stymied at the Kirov and the lives he subsumed: those of Igor Tchernichov, Alla Osipenko, Yuri Soloviev, and Nikita Dolgushin. The innovative Tchernichov was relegated to the provinces (first to Odessa, then Kuibyshev), at a time when the Kirov needed new talent desperately. No ballet was ever created for Alla Osipenko, whose rare and aristocratic lines come along once a century in the dance. She left the Kirov for Leonid Yakobson's little troupe (formed in the mid-sixties) and its dance experiments. Nikita Dolgushin, an unusual example of a Romantic intellectual dancer, also had to try to realize his potential outside the Kirov, on the provincial stage in Siberia and in Leningrad's Maly theater.

Now Sergeyev would in turn be dismissed. By leading the fight against him, Irina Kolpakova vindicated the artists who had suffered the effects of his absolutism more than she. But nothing could stop the Kirov's deterioration. In a sense, it crowned the whole dismal picture of Soviet reprisals against Russian culture. The Kirov ballet was the last page in the history of its extermination.

By 1970 the old keepers of the St. Petersburg ballet traditions at the Vaganova School had died. Many of the experienced professors had retired. Sergeyev was appointed the school's artistic director, but even his professionalism could not save a desperate situation. At the school's annual graduation performances, the young dancers looked devastatingly colorless, poor replacements for the array of talent which had filled the Kirov stage in the nineteen-fifties and -sixties, whose artistic potential had been so misused. Of that group, only those who defected survived.

No administrative measures seemed to help. The triumvirate which took Sergeyev's place in 1971 (composed of Irina Kolpakova, Vladilen Semenov, and Oleg Vinogradov) reigned briefly. In their attempts to rescue the sinking ship, they acted without coordination, aggravating the situation. Nobody at the Kirov relished this interregnum. (Though, to Kolpakova's satisfaction, her husband was finally awarded the title of Honored Artist of Soviet Russia.) The hapless co-directors were replaced by 1973 by Igor Belsky, who until then had headed the Maly theater, also in shambles. Belsky had been a gifted character dancer at the Kirov in the fifties. Since then he had created a decent Soviet drama ballet, *Coast of Hope* (1959), and his awkward *Leningrad Symphony* was performed in New York in 1961. Various incoherent compositions followed.

Hiring Belsky only made things worse. If Sergeyev at least enjoyed a certain professional respect, none of Belsky's colleagues took him seriously. He in turn chose to play the part of a goodhearted, garrulous buffoon, a light-opera role inappropriate to the veritable tragedy at hand. He might have believed that it was not possible to stop the Kirov's decline—his tenure had the desperate gaiety of a feast during the plague. Sometimes his attitude became grotesque, his wit derisive. During a performance of *Legend of Love*, after Act I a major dance critic complained to Belsky that the principal dancer, Valentina Ganibalova, as Mekhmene-Banu, did not even seem to know the order of the steps she sloppily performed. He cheerfully replied, "You're kidding. She's wonderful in Act I. Wait, angel, until you see her pranks in Act II."

Misha never concealed his poor opinion of Belsky. When Belsky began to work on *Icarus*, a ballet set to Sergei Slonimsky's music, he refused point-blank to participate in what could only be a "programmed fiasco."

In 1974, the game of administrative leapfrog continued, and Oleg Vinogradov returned to take over the Kirov's direction. At that time,

With Igor Belsky / N. SLEZINGER

Baryshnikov was despondent over his attempts to arrange his own successful solo performance or "creative evening."

In the mid-sixties, the idea of "creative evenings" took hold at the Kirov. Performances were organized around one dancer; the evenings were diverse and included a series of short pieces, choreographic miniatures and one-act ballets. The dancer himself selected the program, the music, and the choreographers, often in opposition to the will of the Kirov management. The performances were given, as a rule, only a few times (occasionally, just once), so that the danger of some enigmatic tropical plant taking root in the classical Kirov garden was minimal. For the young, usually non-conformist choreographers, and even for those who were established, these evenings were a way into real art, a rare opportunity to get something of the self onto the official stage. From the management's point of view, these artists were given just enough freedom to keep them from choking to death. And the programs were evidence, before the all-seeing eye of the West, that the Kirov encouraged experimentation.

These ephemeral productions were let out like exotic beasts on long leashes, and after being viewed, they were pulled back into the dark. But it was thanks to these evenings that the public had a glimpse of various seditious works, such as Yakobson's *Repenting Magdalen* (Kaleria Fedicheva's evening) and *A Passing Beauty*, as performed by Natalia Makarova; Tchernichov's pas de deux with music by Honegger and Britten (Fedicheva dancing); his *Bolero* (Ganibalova's evening), and the ill-fated Berlioz *Romeo and Juliet* (Kolpakova's evening). All of these mini-ballets were thus granted a short life on the Kirov stage.

Misha was assigned an evening after he had been accorded the title of Honored Artist of the Republic at the end of 1973. In return, he was expected to prove his worth publicly. He was quite aware of the risks involved, and he himself assumed the responsibility for selecting the program pieces. If it failed, he would have only himself to blame. Moreover, he would not be able to use the excuses applicable to traditional programs—old-fashioned choreography, decrepit scenery, and so on. Misha could easily have put together an evening of approved numbers which would have permitted him to show his stuff, for instance the "Kingdom of the Shades" from *La Bayadère*, or the pas de deux from *Le Corsaire* and *Don Quixote*. But he wanted to dance works produced especially for him, by choreographers who were not in official favor.

In the early seventies these choreographers were tolerated as a sort of fifth column and permitted to work on an occasional piece. They included Tchernichov, Gyorgy Aleksidze, and Mai Murdmaa. Aleksidze was a master of dance miniatures, whose subtle choreography resembled Jerome Robbins's. (Today, Aleksidze heads the Tbilisi Theater of Opera and Ballet in Soviet Georgia.) Murdmaa's somewhat cerebral, cold, yet imaginative ballet compositions showed a strong Scandinavian influence. She received support and encouragement in Tallinn, the capital of her native Estonia, which was hostile to Moscow's edicts. Baryshnikov hoped to collaborate with all three choreographers.

Misha spent the entire winter of 1973–74 preparing for the evening's program, as Mai set about adapting her Tallinn versions of Ravel's *Daphnis and Chloë* and Prokofiev's *The Prodigal Son*. The librettos and scores of both compositions are dramatic and musical gems, and both have an illustrious ballet history. Ravel wrote *Daphnis and Chloë* in 1912, for Mikhail Fokine, who composed the libretto after the Greek novel by Longus. Serge Diaghilev's Saisons Russes ended its final season, in 1929, with *The Prodigal Son*, choreographed by George Balanchine. Both ballets had protagonists perfectly suited to Baryshnikov's physical type. Misha asked Igor Tchernichov if he would do a composition to Brahms's Violin Concerto as the third piece on the program. Together with Kolpakova, his regular partner at the time, Baryshnikov set out for Odessa, where Igor was working as principal choreographer. He was flattered by the proposal, but in a fit of pique at Kolpakova, who had not put his *Romeo and Juliet* into the Kirov repertoire, he decided to take his own brand of revenge on the Kirov stars who had come to pay homage to him in the provinces. Referring to his frenzied schedule, he proposed that they work only late at night. As a result, the days were spent in idleness, and Igor was tired and hurried at rehearsals. Tension reigned, and the collaboration ended in mutual animosity as the two stars departed for Tbilisi—to Gyorgy Aleksidze, another non-conformist Kirov exile.

Misha asked Gyorgy to create a divertissement to *Les Petits Riens*, music Mozart had written for a pantomime performed by the cavalier Jean Georges Noverre. (It premièred at the Paris Opera in 1778.)

The winter turned into an exhausting ordeal. Misha experienced the full force of his colleagues' indifference to his "evening," of their

phnis and Chloë, with Tatiana Koltzova / BLIOKH

The Prodigal Son, with Alla Osipenko / BLIOKH

aesthetic apathy. It seemed only natural that his enthusiasm ought to be shared by the troupe. After all, it was not simply a matter of his own performance but of three new ballets at one time, a rare occurrence at the Kirov. Yet the corps de ballet was undisciplined, unwilling to remain at rehearsal a minute longer than required. Baryshnikov struggled to patch things together somehow, but it seemed that someone always had an excuse to avoid extra rehearsal time. This indifference disheartened Baryshnikov all the more since he himself was working with the choreographers more as a collaborator than as a performer. This sort of intensive cooperation had always been in the best tradition of Russian ballet.

In the case of *Daphnis and Chloë* and *The Prodigal Son*, such cooperation was vital, since both ballets had first been created in Estonia for the *premier danseur* of the Tallinn ballet, Tiit Härm (who studied with Baryshnikov in Pushkin's class). Härm's artistic potential and physical characteristics were entirely different from Misha's; he did not have the same technique, was taller, more statuesque, and less expressive. Murdmaa adapted the works to Baryshnikov's range with difficulty, using more intricate variations and more complex dance resolutions. In rehearsal, Baryshnikov himself often came up with the right movements, and Murdmaa was enthralled by his energy and conscientiousness.

In rehearsing *The Prodigal Son*, another complication arose. The female lead was to be played by Valentina Ganibalova, a competent ballerina whose prima donna whims were unfortunately out of line with her talent and technical abilities. She complained constantly about the awkwardness of the steps and demanded that various movements be changed. She even complained that Baryshnikov possessed no real knack for partnering, and finally dropped out, having succeeded in thoroughly annoying everyone. The break, while it was her doing, embittered her against Baryshnikov. After his defection, she gained notoriety in ballet circles for her disparaging comments. "Why's everyone weeping?" she asked. "We're better off now that he's gone. What was so great about him? He knew how to do good *cabrioles en avant* . . ."

At Misha's request, Ganibalova was replaced by one of the most prized ballerinas in the Kirov theater, Alla Osipenko. In 1973, she was already dancing outside the company, performing a small group of Leonid Yakobson's choreographic miniatures. Osipenko had dazzlingly

beautiful legs and fine lines, as well as a restrained lyricism and coolness that marvelously suited roles like the Lilac Fairy, the Mistress of the Copper Mountain (in Yuri Grigorovich's *The Stone Flower*) or Mekhmene-Banu (in Grigorovich's *Legend of Love*). Displeased with the administration's indifference toward her and her husband, the dancer John Markovsky (well known in the West as the Prince in the Soviet film version of the Kirov's *Swan Lake*), she left the theater (to the immense pleasure of Irina Kolpakova, her constant rival).

Osipenko was already past forty, but she still possessed amazing form and had a strong commitment to work that matched Baryshnikov's. Her discipline was typical of the generation that grew up in the forties under the tutelage of Agrippina Vaganova. At the rehearsals I observed, she would often say things like, "Let's try it again, Misha . . . No, no, it was my fault. I haven't got the choreography down yet . . ." Osipenko was the only partner of Misha's whose artistic passion and demands on herself were no less than his own.

The rehearsals cost Baryshnikov tremendous effort, probably more than any other ballet, and the first dress rehearsal disturbed him greatly. Nothing worked. First of all, the set designer, Svetlana Dmitrieva, was a mediocre artist whose talent was best revealed in portraiture. *Daphnis and Chloë*, the ancient Greek lovers' pastoral tryst, unfolded against a backdrop depicting an Arcadian landscape with rather pensive, realistically drawn sheep. Pale blues and pinks and Empire curlicues for *Mozartiana* (as *Les Petits Riens* was finally called) were out of touch with the composer's seraphic purity and evoked provincial kitsch. The sets for *The Prodigal Son*, compared to those Rouault designed for the Balanchine production—fresh in everyone's mind from the New York City Ballet's first visit to the U.S.S.R. in 1962—looked especially bleak and unimaginative. Moreover, their muddy-green and brown tones gave the ballet an oppressive mood.

Murdmaa's choreography, which had looked so interesting in rehearsal, seemed, in production, to be cut from an altogether different piece of cloth. In *Daphnis, par terre* combinations prevailed. But leaps would have been more appropriate to Baryshnikov's character, that of a sportive shepherd who unwillingly parts with his innocence and gradually comes to know the taste of love. The choreography, which had Baryshnikov rolling about on the floor, disappointed an audience expecting fireworks. Daphnis was too tame a role for Baryshnikov—there was no drama in it, and no comedic play. Misha fluttered about

◁ Moving into his first comfortable apartment / N. SLEZINGER

the stage diligently with his Chloë (Tatiana Koltzova), trying to compensate with charm for what the choreography lacked. Murdmaa made dynamic use of space, but her principles seemed too self-consciously derived from Fokine's. The choreography looked imitative, dated.

Her *Prodigal Son* would have been much more convincing had it not been seen in the shadow of Balanchine's chef d'oeuvre. There, the majesty of the biblical parable combined with a touching story in which picturesque elements à la Fokine or Kasyan Goleizovsky were ironically set off and juxtaposed against bold, more abstract dance compositions. By contrast, Murdmaa's version eliminated realistic, everyday details and all graphic pantomime, constructing the ballet as a pure dance accompaniment to Prokofiev's music. Unluckily, her approach did not correspond to the music at all.

In spite of its symphonic structure, Prokofiev's score was conceived for a drama ballet combining both pantomime and pure dance selections. Balanchine's choreography was true to that balance, while Murdmaa's attempt to create a pure dance ballet was simply wrong. The choreography could not be perceived as a pure metaphor, since it had to serve a dramatic purpose. The plot imposed itself anyway. No matter how intricate the combinations, Murdmaa's choreography remained fundamentally illustrative. What's more, the baby was thrown out with the bath water—without the pantomime, the flavor of the biblical fable totally disappeared. The ballet became instead a banal story about a crazy lad who, after a series of unlucky escapades, returns to his forgiving daddy. And although Baryshnikov's dancing was exemplary, even stunning, the lack of dramatic consistency affected it, and no amount of artistry could compensate for the choreographic problems.

Aleksidze's *Mozartiana* turned out to be the most successful piece of the evening. This charming ballet, filled with Balanchinian touches, revealed both the choreographer's musicality and his understanding of Misha's needs as a dancer. Misha performed a virtuoso solo, and all its beats and splits, with a special lightness and elegance; a touch of *Vestris* suddenly reappeared in this variation, a half-serious, half-ironical attitude toward the dancing that matched the spirit of Mozart's musical bagatelle. Baryshnikov's dancing was the music's plastic metaphor.

After the preview, I dropped by Misha's apartment, where some friends had gathered. He looked upset, clearly disappointed with his creative evening. Energy and time, he felt, had been wasted to no purpose, "as if I had tried to turn fish soup into an aquarium." I did not want to pour salt into open wounds by discussing the evening, but he broached the subject himself and we analyzed the performance's shortcomings. "Well," he summarized, "I tried my best. It's not my fault that I joined the company when it was falling apart."

The following performances only confirmed our critical evaluation. Baryshnikov's artistry went beyond his material, though he tried to make the best of the situation. The critics praised him as an absolute master, but the shadow of failure seemed to hover over him and most of the performances he danced in the spring of 1974.

I had not seen him for a couple of months but had heard he was depressed, rarely went out, and killed his spare evenings with boon companions. The Kirov routine, devoid of any radiant perspectives, was becoming unbearable. Misha revealed his despondency when I called him one evening. "What are you going to say? That life is wonderful, that I am a marvelous dancer and shouldn't give up? . . . I'm fed up to the brim."

After this talk on the phone, on April 30, 1974, I saw his *Giselle* with Bessmertnova, which turned out to be his last performance at the Kirov. Baryshnikov had never portrayed his daydreaming Albrecht

With friends in a Leningrad apartment
/ N. SLEZINGER

with more dramatic color, never looked so vulnerable or so desperate. An Italian friend of mine who was seeing Baryshnikov for the first time suddenly said to me afterward, "He definitely has to live in the West. He is suffocated here." I suggested he try to persuade Misha of this and half seriously offered to arrange a meeting. "Nobody should persuade him. He will understand it himself." I was not so optimistic, since I knew Misha would be unsure about pulling up all roots, hesitant about making such a sacrifice. And I wondered aloud if Misha's tremendous potential could ever be fully realized, even in the West.

"That's hardly the point," my friend continued. "Soviet reality deprives you of vitality, free choice. It's comfortable when everything is decided for you, but you have to pay for that with the paralysis of your mind and will. When Misha is ready for freedom, his frustration will prompt him to make the right decision. He will leave Russia . . . Remember my words."

I did not believe him.

A FTER THE DISAPPOINTMENT of his solo performance, Baryshnikov, understandably restless at twenty-six, began to consider alternatives. More and more frequently, he would allude to them in conversation: "What if I just went to the Ministry and said to Demichev [the Minister of Culture], 'Let me go abroad to dance, for half a year—with Roland Petit, or the Stuttgart Ballet, for instance. I agree to work for the smallest percentage and will spend the rest of the year at the Kirov. Is this not reasonable? I won't run off, my place is here!'"

Such a proposal would have been unlikely to get Misha very far. There were constant rumors that he would follow Makarova, and he was too young and too talented for the KGB to risk losing. For the KGB official who signed the permission slip, Baryshnikov's defection would mean losing a good salary, free vacations, excursions abroad, and other special privileges unavailable to ordinary citizens. Vladimir Vasiliev and Maya Plisetskaya were permitted to work with Maurice Béjart and allowed extensive independent travel in the West only in the seventies, when their careers were coming to a close.

If Baryshnikov had been allowed to go to the West legally, he would probably not have sought political asylum there. He was deeply rooted in Russian culture, and he had strong personal attachments in Leningrad and Moscow. Besides, Baryshnikov was not convinced that his career would go smoothly in the West. The transition to a more varied repertoire might prove difficult, and Misha was not sure he could adapt.

In the winter of 1974, Roland Petit came to Leningrad with his Marseilles troupe. Earlier, in December 1968, his *Notre-Dame de Paris*, beautifully danced by the Paris Opera company, had created a sensation in Moscow. We had never seen such a refined neoclassical synthesis, such a fine stylization of the Middle Ages as in Yves Saint Laurent's costumes, or such a brilliant ensemble—Claire Motte as Esmeralda, Jean-Pierre Bonnefous as Phoebus, Jean-Pierre Franchetti as Claude, and the amazing Cyril Atanassoff as Quasimodo. This time, *Notre-Dame*, a bit tarnished but still impressive, *Carmen*, and *L'Arlésienne* completely conquered the snobbish Leningrad audience.

Baryshnikov was no less enthralled than the others. Petit and Baryshnikov met at the tour's opening performance of *Notre Dame*, which received a tremendous ovation. But Roland Petit himself was clearly applauding Baryshnikov, who was sitting in the first row. He had seen him in class and had been staggered by Baryshnikov's purity of form and elegance of execution. They became friends that winter, and once, after a rehearsal, Misha invited Roland and his wife, Zizi Jeanmaire, to have supper with him at home.

Baryshnikov was then living in a comfortable apartment, charmingly furnished, located on the Moika Canal, right across from the great poet Alexander Pushkin's last apartment, in one of Leningrad's most picturesque nooks. The supper was thoroughly appropriate to the old Petersburg setting—fresh black caviar, cold veal in lingonberry sauce, marinated white mushrooms, fine Georgian wine, and Armenian cognac. I helped with the animated conversation, which was partially in French and had Igor Belsky looking quite lost. Misha sensed this and felt uncomfortable for his boss.

After supper, we walked Roland and Zizi back to the Evropeiskaya Hotel. Roland took advantage of the fact that Misha was strolling somewhat behind us with Zizi and his huge, shaggy white poodle, Foma. He asked me point-blank if Misha was planning to remain in Europe after the coming tour. (The Kirov was supposed to go to Italy.) I replied that he would be unlikely to tell anyone, including me, of plans to leave, but that he had seemed hesitant whenever the idea came up.

"That's crazy. With his fantastic talent, sitting around at the Kirov is simply suicide—he'll choke on the routine," Roland remarked.

"Tell him that. Maybe he'll listen to you," I said. "You could stage some marvelous things for him. What about *Daughters of Fire* after Gérard de Nerval's writing or *The Queen of Spades* set to Tchaikovsky's opera music?"

Roland responded that he did not think *The Queen of Spades* would lend itself to the ballet medium with the same ease as *Carmen*, for instance, since Bizet wrote divertissements, while Tchaikovsky used a symphonic structure. But he thanked me for the idea.

On the way back, I told Misha about my talk with Petit. He continued to justify his remaining in Russia, citing the *commedia dell'arte* ballet Yakobson was planning for him. But the *Queen of Spades* idea intrigued him. He thought of inviting Petit to stage the ballet for him at the Kirov, and they did, in fact, take the project on in 1978, after Misha's defection.

Misha's meeting with Roland, and the thought of working with him on *The Queen of Spades*, may well have been small catalysts in his

With Foma and cat in Leningrad apartment / N. SLEZINGER

decision to leave Russia. In any case, during the spring of 1974, he seemed to have defection on his mind. I recall him asking me, "Do you think that if I worked, let's say, in New York, I'd be successful?"

"I guarantee you that in a couple of months you'd be a superstar," I answered. (I was wrong. Baryshnikov became a superstar after just a few performances with the American Ballet Theatre.)

Though our conversations often referred indirectly to the possibility of his leaving, his unexpected telephone call caught me by surprise. Baryshnikov was asking me to coach him in a bit of conversational French.

"Why French?" I asked ingenuously. "You'd be better off studying English."

"No, they're talking about a little trip to Canada, and I don't want to look like a bleating sheep there."

Several years later, after I, too, had arrived in New York, I reminded Misha of that conversation. I asked him if he really hadn't gotten my hint when I suggested he study English. He swore he hadn't, and wasn't even thinking of America at the time.

Although we had only a few lessons, due to busy schedules, I was struck by the swiftness with which Misha grasped French grammar. He made a game of soaking up idioms, quickly mastered the Parisian accent, and would greet me with a stream of expressions as I opened the door. Baryshnikov's linguistic talent served him well in the United States. He arrived with just a handful of phrases, but by watching television and constantly speaking to Americans, he immediately acquired an enviable facility for the spoken language—something Russian emigré dancers are not noted for.

The trip to Canada was scheduled for June. The tour members, a rather sorry lot, were to be overseen by Raissa Struchkova and her husband, Alexander Lapauri. Both, in their day, had made a career in ballet more through Party connections than through talent. Neither was in the prime of life, although Struchkova, who was well past forty, still appeared as *Giselle* from time to time at the Bolshoi. In fact, the little troupe—which included Nicolai Fadeyechev, near retirement, Yaroslav Sekh, an unremarkable soloist, and several mediocre young Bolshoi soloists—was put together with an eye to the participants' loyalty. And although it was supposed to represent the "stars of the Soviet ballet," it had the look of caricature. The program was a potpourri of excerpts and threadbare divertissements from the Bolshoi repertoire—*Walpurgisnacht*, which Russians respected as a specimen of Soviet balletic camp, and which exceeded all the limits of platitude; *Spring Waters*, which had long exasperated Soviet audiences even in the 1950s with its official optimism and banality; a duet called *Dolls*, another leftover; the second act of *Swan Lake*, in the awkward Gorsky version; the pas de deux from Act II of *Giselle*, decently adapted by Leonid Lavrovsky; and the like.

In order to cover up the program's dullness, invitations were issued to Baryshnikov and Irina Kolpakova. Thanks to her excellent training, Kolpakova continued to manifest miracles of professionalism, though she, too, was past her prime. When she danced Giselle to Baryshnikov's Albrecht on June 6, 1974, at the Bolshoi, she pleasantly surprised those who justifiably considered her talents inappropriate for the role.

For the tour, Misha was to dance a couple of pas de deux from *Don Quixote* with Struchkova and from *The Nutcracker* (Vasily Vainonen's obsolete version) with Irina Kolpakova. Kolpakova's political façade showed no flaws. Baryshnikov's situation was much more vulnerable. Each time he was permitted to go abroad, the KGB ran a risk. In addition, the Kirov's director, the former fireman Rachinsky, was frightened to death by the Panov affair, which had aroused such publicity in the West, and would have preferred that his flock stay home altogether. Kolpakova activated all her connections and, it seems, even guaranteed Baryshnikov's safe return home. Kolpakova's commitment must have tormented Baryshnikov when the time came for his crucial decision in Toronto. He always treated Kolpakova kindly, danced with her gladly, and to this day speaks of her with an admiration that I don't feel she, as a ballerina, fully deserves.

Baryshnikov's trip abroad became the subject of the liveliest gossip in Moscow and Leningrad. Friends wondered if they had seen him dance for the last time. I was afraid to heed my own intuition, which was that he would return. On the eve of his departure, Baryshnikov paid a farewell visit to all his close friends. He arrived at my place in the light-green Volga that he had just gotten and stayed for a few minutes. He was calm, and spoke mostly of his new work with Yakobson and of the tour the Kirov might make to Italy.

I accompanied him down to his car and simply said: "Wise up!"

"I will," he answered as obliquely.

VALERY PLOTNIKOV

Arlene Croce saw him perform in Montreal, and her comments summarized the impressions of many people who saw Baryshnikov dance in North America for the first time:

> He carries the impeccable to the point where it vanishes into the ineffable . . . When he walks out onto the stage, he doesn't radiate—doesn't put the audience on notice that he's a star. His body, with its short, rounded muscles, isn't handsome; he's no Anthony Dowell. His head and hands are large, and his face—pale, peaked features and distant eyes—is the face of Petrouchka . . . Baryshnikov is able to perform unparalleled spectacular feats as an extension of classical rather than character or acrobatic dancing . . . He gets into a step sequence more quickly, complicates it more variously, and prolongs it more extravagantly than any dancer I've ever seen. And he finishes when he wants to, not when he has to. Perhaps his greatest gift is his sense of fantasy in classical gesture. He pursues the extremes of its logic so that every step takes on an unforeseen dimension. His grande pirouette is a rhapsody of swelling volume and displaced weight. He does not turn; he is turned—spun around and around by the tip of his toe . . . Baryshnikov both summarizes and extends the resources of classical expression.

The defection turned out to be pure improvisation, as Baryshnikov still tells it. Of course, were it not for the support of several friends, he would hardly have taken the step which cut him off forever from the possibility of strolling around Leningrad, dropping by the Vaganova School, taking flowers to Pushkin's grave, and sitting down with old friends over a bottle of vodka. That step meant becoming a criminal in the eyes of the law, and was punishable by up to fifteen years in prison. Baryshnikov vacillated for a long time, and even during the last week, right up to his last evening performance on June 29, kept changing his mind. His friends were in a state of desperate suspense.

By the matinee on the twenty-ninth, the legal arrangements had already been carefully taken care of—only Misha's final word was needed. For several hours he and the others were silent, as he paced back and forth in the home of his Canadian friend. Finally, he agreed to make his move after the evening's performance of the *Don Quixote* pas de deux with Raissa Struchkova. For purely professional considerations, he could not disrupt the troupe's last performance before they left Toronto for another city the next day.

Misha tried to telephone Makarova in London, but failed to reach her. She was dancing *Giselle* with the Royal Ballet and was to be in New York several days later for the première of the "Kingdom of the Shades" from *La Bayadère* July 3. He needed her support as an old friend, and her advice in making the decision. She could let him know the likelihood of his dancing in New York with the American Ballet Theatre. ABT was the only New York company performing *Swan Lake*, *Giselle*, and the "Shades" of *La Bayadère*, works he could dance immediately as Makarova's partner.

Baryshnikov left for the theater in a terribly nervous state. He was shaking, and feared that his agitation would awaken the suspicion of the tour's leaders, the Lapauris, who had only to telephone Moscow and Baryshnikov would be removed from the group in the interests of safety. This, in turn, could mean that he might never be able to make a trip to the West again. A case in point was Valery Panov, who, like Kafka's Josef K., had tried for fifteen years to find out what he had done wrong in America to keep him tied to the Kirov stage ever since. Panov's example was doubly disturbing for the ferocity with which the KGB reacted when he decided to emigrate to Israel. The prediction "Panov will leave Russia in a wheelchair" spread through Leningrad and was well known to Baryshnikov. Be that as it may, Misha told his friends that he would meet them in a restaurant near the theater right after the performance, whereupon they would take him to a safe place.

Misha's friends finally managed to reach Makarova. She was ready and willing to help, and the participants in the affair later never tired of repeating her words: "Look into his eyes, and if they are the same blue and just as pure—then turn yourselves inside out, but do everything you can for him."

In his last performance with Soviet dancers, Baryshnikov was especially inspired and technically brilliant. According to Karen Kain, then a principal dancer with the National Ballet of Canada, the hall literally roared in ecstasy. Meanwhile, something had gone wrong with the curtain (a lift had broken), and the performance had begun somewhat late. The *Don Quixote* pas de deux was last, and Misha appeared on stage at exactly 10:30. His friends were going out of their minds in the restaurant, not knowing what to think. After the performance, there was to be a farewell party in Toronto. The Lapauris announced to Baryshnikov that his presence was obligatory and that they would be waiting for him with a car in front of the backstage door.

After the curtain call, Baryshnikov flew into his dressing room, got dressed, and dashed for the exit. There was a crowd of admirers there waiting for autographs, and Baryshnikov plunged straight into their midst. This made the operation easier. Had he bumped into Lapauri or any of the other Soviet brass, it would have been psychologically much more difficult for him to break away. So he used the crowd for cover, desperately pushing forward. From the car, he could hear

selle, with Natalia Makarova / DINA MAKAROVA

cries of "Misha, where are you going?" He shot back over his shoulder that he was going to the corner to say goodbye to some friends and would be right back. Baryshnikov broke into a run, the crowd behind him. Crossing the street, he was almost run over by a passing car. He pushed on without a destination, getting farther and farther ahead of his fans. As luck would have it, disturbed by Baryshnikov's being so late, one of his friends had set out for the theater to find out what was causing the delay. Misha was racing down the street toward him like a crazy man, shaking with excitement. The friend put him in a taxi and they headed for a private apartment where they would be safe. Later everyone got deliriously drunk—and Baryshnikov requested political asylum in Canada. He was terribly excited, laughing out of control one moment, melancholy the next. That night, the twenty-ninth of June, he finally reached Makarova on the phone. Natalia promised him that as soon as she arrived in New York (she was leaving the next day) she would talk with Lucia Chase about several performances with herself and ABT for that season.

The July 3 première of the "Kingdom of the Shades" was naturally out of the question—he would not be able to obtain immigration papers in time, about a three-week process. But the season's only performance of *Giselle* was coming up on the twenty-seventh of July, and Makarova promised it to Baryshnikov. She was counting on her scheduled partner, Ivan Nagy, to understand the exceptional circumstances and give the part to Misha. Ivan did not disappoint her, and on July 27, 1974, Baryshnikov made his debut in New York.

The official approval for political asylum in Canada did not come until July 2 (June 29 was a Saturday), and the formalities would take another three weeks. Meanwhile, since Baryshnikov was in Canada, the National Ballet of Canada felt that his first night in the West should be with them. But the troupe at the time was on tour in New York, presenting Rudolf Nureyev's new staging of *The Sleeping Beauty*.

In order not to offend the Canadians, Baryshnikov's newly acquired manager was negotiating for him to dance the Blue Bird in *The Sleeping Beauty* with Makarova, meanwhile well aware that Rudi—dancing Prince Florimund—would not be likely to permit it. Nureyev had significantly broadened the role of the prince (even going against Tchaikovsky's score by appropriating some of the music for the Lilac Fairy's variation). In this way, Nureyev had brought the extremely tentative prince to the foreground.

As might be expected, the idea of Baryshnikov as the Blue Bird did not go over. Misha lived outside town, attending class once a day. When the journalists sniffed out his whereabouts and started lying in wait for him outside the house, Baryshnikov's friends moved him to an island. There, after daily exercise, he would take up his favorite pastime—fishing. This always calmed him down and, for the first few weeks after the defection, was absolutely necessary for him. He was tortured by the thought that there was no way back to Russia; insomnia and nightmares troubled his sleep; he broke out in a rash. The invitation from Canadian television to perform Bournonville's *La Sylphide* (a work he had not danced before) came just at the right time. Baryshnikov needed an emotional safety valve, and as always, he found it in work.

To assimilate Bournonville's style presented no particular difficulty. The minor technique of little slides, beats, and *brisés* in combination with high but not soaring leaps on which it is based came to Misha immediately. He felt sure of himself in the classical style of Petipa and the Romantic style of *Giselle*, by comparison with which *La Sylphide* was archaic. The role of James excited him, though it did not involve any complex problems of interpretation. And after Albrecht, James looked more like a Romantic watercolor done in sure but somewhat pale colors. The role had little by way of range for an actor's fantasy or for a psychological approach. Therefore, the basic problem that Baryshnikov set for himself was a stylistic one—nuances and overtones emerged later in the process of work on the role on stage at ABT.

Having danced *La Sylphide* successfully on Canadian television, Baryshnikov arrived in New York.

The performance of *Giselle* had aroused considerable anticipation on the part of Natalia Makarova's fans. She is, after all, the best Giselle of our day. The tickets for the performance at the New York State Theater were almost all sold (there were only ninety seats left) when the news spread that her partner would be Baryshnikov. Lines quickly swelled into crowds outside the theater, police lines were broken, and the remaining tickets disappeared in a flash. Such hullabaloo, usual on the Russian scene but quite unheard-of in America, was something that even the ballet old-timers had not seen before.

G_ISELLE_ MARKED THE BEGINNING of Baryshnikov's ballet marathon in the West. He made his New York debut, not in a show-stopping excerpt like the pas de deux from _Le Corsaire_ or _Don Quixote_, but in an essentially mime and partnering role which placed the choreographic emphasis on the ballerina. After his debut Anna Kissel-goff concisely pointed out in _The New York Times_ the special qualities of Baryshnikov as a unique classical dancer:

> There are two types of great male dancers. Some do not conceal the heroic preparation and effort involved in the most demanding virtuoso feats and derive their very impact from this exciting climax—of difficulties visibly surmounted. Then there are those who purposely strive to go beyond technique and, concentrating on stylistic purity, conceal their own virtuosity.
>
> Mr. Baryshnikov, as he has shown in the past and now in his two brief solos in Act II, is a unique blend of both types. The extraordinary difficulty of the steps he executed (such as the double assemblé that only less than a handful of dancers in the world can do) was evident. At the same time, while the virtuosity was visible, it appeared to be without effort.
>
> Above all, there was a consistency of classical style at every instant that will truly be Mr. Baryshnikov's own special contribution to male dancing in the West.
>
> It is common for many good male dancers to lose their line—that is, to drop out of the correct body position, while moving or jumping. Yet Mr. Baryshnikov's placement is so correct that even when he moves he retains this classroom ideal and transmutes it into artistry.
>
> This was most obvious in his Act II solo, where it is impossible to describe his performance without resorting to ballet terms. All the steps in the air—cabrioles (beats), the double assemblé, the double turns in the air into fifth position, the double turns in the air in the attitude position—were performed with perfect line, pointed and stretched feet in addition to a natural elevation or jump and with a minimum of preparation for the step. At times the State Theater's stage was simply too small for Mr. Baryshnikov.

Makarova was thrilled by their partnership. After the Paris scandal with Rudolf Nureyev at the Palais du Louvre in the summer of 1973,

With Gelsey Kirkland in Washington, D.C. / DINA MAKAROVA

when he dropped her during the pas de deux from *Swan Lake*, their relationship had cooled, precluding future collaboration. So Baryshnikov's appearance as a partner was especially desirable. "We have complete communication. It's very difficult to find a dancer like Baryshnikov. He suits me so much. It's like a marriage," she stated happily.

For Natalia, Misha's appearance in the West was like a breath of fresh air; her feeling of loneliness had been getting worse. Her association with Vladimir Rodzianko, her ill-starred manager from 1970 through 1972, had collapsed completely. Her relationship with her future husband, Edward Karkar, was just beginning, spurred in a complex fashion by her love for Anthony Dowell, who could promise her only friendship at best. In Makarova's mind, Misha was connected with recollections of the only unselfish and passionate love affair that she had had in Russia. At the time, Misha had been a twenty-year-old boy. He arrived in the West a man, mature and sure of what he had left Russia for. Natalia was pleasantly surprised at how he had developed as a partner (in Russia they had danced only *Mountain Girl* together).

But their relationship did not turn out the way she wanted. Natalia expected him to play his former role of a *chevalier servant* devoted to her every whim, always on call as her partner. Misha could not fulfill these expectations, and her demands became constraining. Misha valued Makarova most highly as a partner, but he also wanted to dance with Gelsey Kirkland, probably the American ballerina best suited to him. Gelsey left the New York City Ballet to dance with Misha, and her sacrifice naturally created a certain responsibility for him. They were also involved romantically, which exacted an emotional price and limited Misha's ability to be ready at a moment's notice to dance whatever Makarova wished.

Misha's new life was attended by many of the psychological difficulties experienced by a majority of the Russians transplanted to American soil. Freedom of choice means making decisions and taking responsibility for them. In the Soviet Union, choices are imposed on the individual by the state, and it is easy to justify failure with the excuse that you were never given a chance. Western life, by comparison, offers frequent opportunities, and does not allow you to attribute personal failure to anyone but yourself.

Baryshnikov's first half year in the West was thus unusually de-

Exercising with Natalia Makarova and their coach, Jurgen Schneider (above) / DINA
MAKAROVA American Ballet Theatre rehearsal (right) / PHOTO © BY LEONID LUBIANITSKY

manding. Ballet's new idol after just three performances, he felt a huge responsibility to his audiences. They were eager for a demonstration of his remarkable gifts at every performance, and he could not disappoint them. Soon he was feverishly dancing the new ballets he had been starved for in Russia. Through all this, he missed Russia desperately. He had left close friends behind, many of whom also wanted to leave and were counting on his assistance. Baryshnikov felt guilty for having "saved himself" while his friends remained, and he generously helped those who did get out.

In his first years in the West, Misha's Russian past functioned as a harsh censor to his actions. In interviews, he did not permit himself any criticism of the Soviet state. Unwilling to attribute political meaning to his activities, he was also anxious to protect his father from possible unpleasantness. (It was almost five years before he broke that silence on television's *60 Minutes*: "It is impossible to live in a country where people lie to each other every day.") He thought constantly of one day returning to Russia—though he hardly knew how or for how long—and wished he might "walk invisibly around Leningrad streets, see that it's all much worse, and be cured of nostalgia."

The rather eerie Russian reaction to Misha's flight contributed to his uneasiness. His defection, unlike that of Makarova, was glossed over. The KGB pretended that nothing had happened, and no repressive wave swept the Kirov. This was primarily because the theater bore no formal responsibility in the matter and had even opposed Baryshnikov's going abroad. The decision had been Moscow's. Irina Kolpakova, who had vouched for Baryshnikov's return, defended herself boldly to the KGB. She told them that she could hardly have led him around like a chained bear at a carnival and that she had never intended to perform their work for them anyway. Only the Lapauris were punished, forbidden ever to leave the country. Alexander did not suffer this restriction long: a year later he got drunk at a party, drove into a lamp post, and was killed.

Instead of revealing the truth that Misha had defected, the KGB circulated rumors that he was on an extended professional stay abroad. His fans childishly believed in his imminent return, especially since the rumors stressed Baryshnikov's disappointment with the level of Western ballet. These stories surfaced so frequently that I, like many others, even sent Misha a letter through American journalist friends urging him not to come back.

As if playing on Baryshnikov's nostalgia, the KGB kept his apartment and his belongings in perfect order during his first year in the West. A voice would answer when Misha's knowing friends telephoned his place as a joke. In short, the KGB was playing a sinister game of intimidation.

Misha's period of adjustment was brightened in the fall of 1974 when he met Remi Saunder, who gradually became his most devoted friend in the West. Born in Moscow, Remi left Russia in the thirties as a little girl, accompanied by her mother. Her father was forced to remain and was later killed in the infamous KGB prison, the Lubyanka. Remi spent her youth in perpetual flight—first from Stalin, then from Hitler—until her family settled in America in the early forties. Her own experience as a Russian emigrée and her long-standing friendship with the famous cellist Mstislav Rostropovich and his family (who had

With Alexander Galich, Galina Vishnevskaya-Rostropovich, Mstislav Rostropovich, and Joseph Brodsky at a party for Galich in New York / PHOTO © BY LEONID LUBIANITSKY

left Russia in the seventies) enabled her to understand the psychological and actual problems facing Baryshnikov.

Soviet emigrés often have trouble reading social behavior, or perceiving people's true intentions. This interpretive problem practically never arose for Baryshnikov in Russia, because he and the intelligentsia to which he belonged knew the enemy—the totalitarian power. Their resistance to the state cemented the bond between them, variously

In Georgia, after his 1975 injury / PHOTO © BY LEONID LUBIANITSKY

substituting for or reinforcing emotional ties. Many perceived their membership in this subversive group as a sort of identity.

Remi helped Baryshnikov reorient himself in the West. Their friendship grew into strong mutual affection. To some extent, she replaced his mother, whose absence he had felt so painfully since his adolescence. And being able to speak Russian with her diffused Misha's tension.

Baryshnikov's transition was proving less and less traumatic, though it was marred by an injury suffered on his tour in Australia. In February 1975, on stage at the Sydney Opera House, his ankle buckled after he had successfully landed from a high jump in the *Don Quixote* pas de deux. He had severely sprained his left foot—his most serious injury to date. Despite intense pain, Misha rose and improvised a step with which to continue: he reversed the final series of double and triple pirouettes that complete the piece, shifting his weight onto the right leg. Only then did he dare to glance at his foot, which was swelling rapidly. He froze where he finished, remained there through two curtain calls, and fainted.

Five weeks of rest, swimming, and warm Jacuzzi baths were prescribed. As soon as the swelling began to subside and Misha learned to use crutches, he left Sydney to recuperate at White Oak, a gorgeous 5,500-acre plantation straddling the Florida-Georgia border. It was owned by his friend Howard Gilman, whose apartment Misha shared when in New York. At the plantation he strolled through the woods, fished, and took his first riding lessons. By March 1975 he was ready to continue his dance marathon.

He pounced omnivorously on his new repertoire, as the list of his ballet premières from 1974 through 1976 demonstrates.

1974:	July 27	*Giselle*
	August 5	*La Bayadère* (the "Kingdom of the Shades")*
	August 9	*Don Quixote* (pas de deux)
	October 27	*Coppélia**
	October 30	*Theme and Variations**
	December 26	*Les Patineurs**
	December 28	*La Fille Mal Gardée**
1975:	January 4	*La Sylphide**
	January 9	*Le Jeune Homme et la Mort**

* New ballets in his repertoire.

January 11	*Le Corsaire* (pas de deux)
May 20	*Vestris*
July 23	*Shadowplay**
September 22	*Le Pavillon d'Armide* (pas de quatre)*
September 22	*Le Spectre de la Rose* (Hamburg)*
December 31	*Le Spectre de la Rose* (New York)
September 26	*Swan Lake* (National Ballet of Canada)*
October 22	*Romeo and Juliet* (Royal Ballet, London)*
October 27	*Swan Lake* (Royal Ballet, London)*
December 30	*Awakening**
1976: January 6	*Hamlet Connotations**
January 9	*Push Comes to Shove**
January 13	*Medea**
May 9	*Other Dances**
May 11	*Pas de "Duke"**
June 15	*The Sleeping Beauty*
June 21	*Petrouchka**
June 21	*Le Sacre du Printemps**
July 12	*Once More, Frank**

Baryshnikov at Work handsomely recorded this slew of accomplishments, and leafing through finished copies, Misha remarked with some pride: "The total is twenty-six roles within two years. Not bad for a beginning. In Russia such an achievement would cover my entire artistic life." Later, he would dance a total of twenty-two roles in fifteen months with the New York City Ballet, and declare it worth the effort.

By compressing so many roles into so few months, Misha defied the dancer's greatest enemy, time, by forestalling its debilitating effects. Because aging necessarily affects a dancer's technique, those who have maintained a balance between technique and artistic presence have the advantage. In most cases the strength of a dancer's presence derives from psychological needs. Makarova imbues her heroines with her own fantasies and the fluctuations of her moods. Each performance for her involves self-discovery and self-exploration. She is invariably concerned with finding emotional truth in a performance, no matter how elusive that truth may be.

Rudolf Nureyev shares this concern. Especially in his dancing prime, his passion for movement, and even his passion for life, suffused ballet's usually formal language with sex appeal. That he never was a "neat" dancer constituted an additional challenge, spurring him on to eliminate his imperfections. His involvement in his roles was emotionally satisfying and absolute. Both Makarova and Nureyev exemplified and justified what was essentially the Russian approach to classical ballet as dance drama.

Baryshnikov's case was more complicated. His impeccable artistry became, in the confines of the classical repertoire, a kind of burden. During his Russian period he constantly suffered from the discrepancies between his potential and the limited possibilities of the classical heritage. On the one hand, his technique was only partially realized in ballets like *Giselle* and *Swan Lake*. These Romantic and post-Romantic ballets had been designed as perfect vehicles for the ballerina, but excluded male virtuosity. Misha's almost overpolished brilliance demanded another type of vehicle. No wonder, then, that he chose to reincarnate an eighteenth-century figure and a symbol of male virtuosity, Auguste Vestris.

Baryshnikov, as a perfect product of Russian schooling, couldn't help but share the Russian approach to ballet as dance drama. Like generations of Russian, and especially Soviet, dancers, he had been educated in the traditions of pantomime and so-called balletic realism— a contradiction in terms. Generations performed the same ballets, varying their interpretations and their "moral message," and concerned above all with the psychological approach to a balletic character, its realistic justification. This approach seems to combine sensitivity and an inclination to overdramatize, to deliver a message. It derives from the Russian idea of art as morally purifying, or cathartic.

When Marius Petipa came to Russia from Paris in 1847, he was puzzled by Russian resistance to illogical or contrived ballet plots. The Russians' realistic approach bemused him: what kind of dramatic consistency would they be seeking in ballet which, unlike the theater, depended on fairy tale or melodrama? And what kind of dramatic or moral message could a formal classical step carry, if it were merely a component of a divertissement meant only to delight? But Petipa's idea of classical ballet as a poem written by a dancing body is basically alien to the Russian mind.

Unlike Natalia Makarova, France's Carlotta Grisi, the first Giselle, did not torment herself with moral speculations about whether she should forgive Albrecht or not. Nor was she puzzled by the incongruities of *Giselle*'s plot, which later seemed absurd to the young Russian Alexandre Benois in his *Reminiscences of Russian Ballet*: "It is strange that a perfectly healthy young girl should become insane and die for the sole reason that she discovered her lover's betrayal. The Wilis themselves, who are supposed to be maidens punished after death for having danced too much on earth, sound most implausible. It seems extraordinary there should be so many of these sinful damsels as if there had ever been an epidemic of dancing in that quiet little corner of Germany . . ." Grisi's contemporaries childishly believed in this fairy tale's consistency and took its fantastic incongruities at face value. Russian dancers have always been wary of fantasy, and this skepticism deepened in the twentieth century.

Baryshnikov was the first great Russian dancer in the West to feel, perhaps not even consciously, that this realistic approach, though dramatically effective, did not compel him intellectually. He performed his great classical roles to reinforce his status as superstar, but his inner dissatisfaction only increased. The more he danced James in *La Sylphide*, Solor in the "Kingdom of the Shades," Albrecht in *Giselle*, or Prince Siegfried in both versions of *Swan Lake* (Erik Bruhn's modernized one with the National Ballet of Canada and the traditional one with the Royal Ballet in London), the more he seemed to be conscious of the limits of the Russian approach. These roles, no matter how brilliantly performed, sounded the coda to his Kirov period.

After his last performance in Russia, a year and a half went by (June 1974–December 1975) before I saw Baryshnikov dance again, in *Giselle* with Gelsey Kirkland. This was the American Ballet Theatre's opening production of its 1975–76 season at the Uris Theater. "Don't faint at the scenery and corps," Misha warned me over the telephone. "Or at the peasant pas de deux, which looks like a circus act. But Gelsey's marvelous, quite different from Natalia, very untraditional. Today I'll dance in memory of the Kirov and our conversations on the ballet."

Giselle was indeed a big disappointment, since I was used to the Kirov's academic approach. There was no *port de bras* in the angular, unromantic corps de ballet. Akira Endo conducted Adam so briskly that the music sounded like a cancan. (Adam was a blood relation of Offenbach's.) But Gelsey and Misha were fascinating and convincing. After hundreds of performances in New York and other parts of the world, Misha had changed. His body had lost some of its youthful flesh; his muscles had become more elastic and more defined, his technique sharper. Perhaps some of the earlier smoothness was gone, the fabled Russian legato which had connected his movements. If earlier they had seemed to travel in an unbroken line, that line now sometimes looked dotted. The diagonal open-arm *brisé* toward Myrtha had become even more sensational, as had his high, springy *jeté entrelacé*. But strangely enough, his perfect execution looked just a bit automatic, as if the Kirov devices had ossified slightly. And if in dancing with Bessmertnova in 1974 he had given rein to his feelings or his theatrical instincts in the Russian manner, his flawless mastery now seemed somewhat chilly.

In dancing with Gelsey Kirkland this cool execution was especially well highlighted. She was truly exceptional. At first, her American stamp on the role—a brittle quality that was reminiscent of the young Lillian Gish; the restraint she had developed during her schooling with Balanchine—seemed unconvincing. In the second act, she was at times almost boyishly angular. At others, she seemed at a loss, uncertain of how a spirit ought to behave. But her Gish-like "broken blossom" aspect, her enigmatic quality, marvelously complemented Baryshnikov's similarly reticent but sharp and masterful play. The collision of styles resulted in a drama of two dissimilar beings, as if there were something essential that they hadn't said to each other in the first act, and as if that gap were now irreparable. And thanks to Gelsey's image, the flower symbolism in the second act took on a penetrating lyricism. Théophile Gautier once demanded of the first Giselle, Carlotta Grisi, that she not smile. Gelsey, mostly unsmiling and inscrutable, involuntarily evoked an analogy with Grisi.

Baryshnikov's emotional distance from the role of Albrecht was part of a bigger phenomenon. Misha had respect for the classical roles but did not often identify with them. The unprecedented way Misha's career took shape in the West reflected his need to go beyond what was for him a stale approach. At the peak of his undisputable glory, he preferred to extend his range in modern, sometimes rather controversial choreographic styles, rather than to stagnate in his virtuosity. He was not even afraid of jeopardizing his prestige as a superstar, caring more about fulfillment than about success per se. To a certain degree, he began to struggle against his image as an impeccable virtuoso in order to reveal the human subject, the personality concealed behind his

Giselle, with Gelsey Kirkland / MARTHA SWOPE

show-stopping tricks. Subconsciously he might have been pining for involvement. His new position as a citizen of the world made artistic self-discovery possible.

During his first two years in the West, few if any of the public at large, breathlessly following his rapid, spirited turns on stage, or the wonders of his elevation, understood that what they were seeing was, in a way, merely the glittering façade of a superb dancer. Arlene Croce, who regarded him as a "one-man revolution" in ballet, once remarked that "Baryshnikov's dancing is his showmanship. His acting tends to be a cover for his personality, not a revelation of it." He epitomized classical dancing—an art concerned with harmony and proportion in each gesture or pose—and frequently resembled an ideal model come to life. In comparison with Nureyev's sensuality and tempestuousness, Baryshnikov seemed to hold back, remaining within

the boundaries of classicism, which is by nature a far cry from emotional outpouring.

The contrast between the two approaches creates a persistent debate involving aesthetic values. One side values impeccable technique and God-given coordination above all, though it may mean a loss of expressiveness; the other requires emotional and dramatic impact from a dancer, even at the price of uneven or even sloppy technique. It remained to be seen in what direction Misha would move. In 1974 and 1975 he would probably not have been able to answer this question himself.

But life in the West—New York, indispensably nurturing, and his cosmopolitan trajectory through Paris, London, Rome, and Greece—gave him the confidence in his own judgment that had begun to develop in Russia. Unlike many of his compatriots who left Russia, Misha did not cling to his Russian experience. It was as if he feared that his sally into the West would suddenly come to an end, that it had been a temporary gift, and he therefore made up for time lost in Russia with redoubled effort. Every night that he was not performing, he would race to a movie, a musical, or a contemporary ballet, and he read voraciously—books that were unavailable in the Soviet Union, like Solzhenitsyn's *Gulag Archipelago*, or the poetry of Mandelstam, Tsvetaeva, Brodsky, which he can recite from memory by the hour. In the West, he also discovered the works of Vladimir Nabokov.

The intensity with which he absorbed new knowledge was accompanied by a rapid development of taste and an increasing independence of judgment, of which he was at first self-conscious. He assumed

With Romola Nijinska, Nijinsky's widow, Paris, 1975 / PHOTO © BY LEONID LUBIANITSKY

that a ballet dancer ought not to express opinions of the other arts, but his perceptions were often unusually insightful.

"You know, Shalamov's *Kolyma Stories* are better than Solzhenitsyn. More classical, without a trace of provincialism . . ." Or: "Nabokov has fantastic control in his books. When I read *Despair*, I was struck by the part where Felix sees himself from the side. 'I have grown much too used to this outside view of myself, to being both painter and model . . .' Maybe I take it too personally, but that sort of double vision happens to me all the time on stage. One part of me is dancing, the other observing from the side. This control protects you from an overdone, vulgar presentation. You constantly keep yourself under fire, as it were; you watch, with an ironic eye, as if saying: 'Well, well, so you can do it, but don't show it too much.' Nabokov rarely displays his technique, but his prose is masterful. That's the way it should be—be a master but don't show your mastery."

The process of constant control and self-analysis to which Baryshnikov submits rules out any emotional involvement in the roles of the classical repertoire. Unlike Makarova, he doesn't have to find a new emotional key to each performance. For her, there is always an intimate relationship to the role—whether it's Odette or Giselle—and a certain improvisation within the boundaries of the role itself, an improvisation that depends on her personal feelings of the moment.

For Baryshnikov, ballet is not an art of experience; it is high art. As an actor, he is opposed to Stanislavsky's methods, adhering instead to the "presentational" school, to use Stanislavsky's somewhat outmoded terminology. Great singers and dancers have approached the actual manner of presentation differently. Some had to get inside the skin of the character, to prepare internally before going on stage. Chaliapin could stand in the wings smoking and chatting one minute and stun the audience with his tragic figure of Tsar Boris the next. For Maria Callas, full control meant that a performance must be linked to personal identification with the role, whether it was Norma, Violetta, or Medea. The same was true of Anna Pavlova. Maya Plisetskaya could dash about the shops right up to the beginning of a performance, then, barely warming up, go out on stage as the dazzling Odette. Nijinsky is said to have seemed sleepy before the curtain went up. He would wake up in his role, giving rein to his complexes, then retreat again behind his indifferent mask when the curtain fell.

For Baryshnikov, every performance is another test of his mastery, which, like a façade, covers his real personality. His style depends very little on his partners. Of course, with Gelsey Kirkland he may be somewhat protective and tender, while with Makarova he is usually more aggressive—competitive, in the best sense—but nothing can disrupt his internal control. In this regard, his performance in *Giselle* in the winter of 1977 is instructive. Misha replaced the ailing Ivan Nagy as Makarova's partner two hours before curtain time, although they had not rehearsed the ballet together for a year. In the first act, Makarova forgot to bring the second daisy which Albrecht is supposed to pluck to prove whether "he loves me." Baryshnikov simply tossed aside the first flower, which was already crumpled and plucked, as if to say: "Who believes such superstitious nonsense!" This consoling gesture, inducing Giselle to dance with Albrecht, was improvised with such precision that, discussing it afterward, Makarova praised Misha's quick thinking.

Misha's commentary on performing the role of Albrecht on such short notice was characteristic: "This was improvisation within the bounds of an already worked-out role, one polished down to the last detail. Essentially, Natalia and I don't need to rehearse *Giselle*. The movements are the same ones that we do in class. We've already danced *Giselle* so many times that for me each new performance is a special sort of recollection. The body's memory almost subconsciously draws out of somewhere new nuances, which in essence are not really new at all. They have already been done."

Baryshnikov's assessment illustrates one thing clearly: his mastery in *Giselle* and the other classics has grown to the point where it can't be improved. And now, only in the hands of a very inventive director-choreographer, who would interpret these ballets in new ways, can Baryshnikov find exciting dimensions in his roles.

Baryshnikov's struggle against his image of virtuoso dancer of the classics was developing at breakneck speed, corresponding to some extent to the swiftness with which he absorbed everything new in Western culture. In this duel with himself he was motivated by his precious intuition, and at times his decisions puzzled both his manager and his intimate friends. His situation was all the more dramatic since, as he put it himself, "In ballet, choreographers choose you. You do not choose the choreographer, no matter how you may ache to dance in their works. I have been very lucky. But people have gone around saying that I use choreographers—that I want to work with them just

so I can say that I have a whole string of choreographers who wanted to work with me. Well, that's not true. I have never asked a choreographer to create anything for me, even though some of them are close personal friends. For example, Béjart is someone I know very well, but I would never call him and say: 'Listen, Maurice, I need a new ballet. How about creating one for me?' He would think I was crazy. Or take Balanchine. When I came to New York, I was desperately hoping to dance his *Apollo* and *The Prodigal Son*. But it took nearly three years to have that chance . . . I don't think Mr. Balanchine has ever seen me dance his works. I understand this. He is a very busy man . . . The point is that we, as dancers, are only instruments. We cannot make demands . . ."

That's why he used every new opportunity selfishly, concerned with his own need. "Nureyev's example was a great lesson and inspiration for me. He was the first to dare anything, to dance whatever was new and exciting. I have tried to do the same. Every encounter with a new choreographer is like a celebration for me."

But in expanding his repertoire range, Nureyev's approach differed from Baryshnikov's. In whatever style Nureyev was experimenting, he tried to outdo himself as an electrifying personality and technical virtuoso. To a certain extent, he subjugated the styles to his forte. Baryshnikov, on the other hand, seemed to eschew his forte—his classical virtuosity and Russian theatricality. He not only explored the new possibilities of his body; he somehow fostered a new attitude toward ballet per se, shifting in at least two seemingly contradictory directions toward an impersonal style in which the dancing body is a pure metaphor, and simultaneously to a more profound understanding of restrained emotional projection.

His first forays into impersonal style were in *Les Patineurs* by Frederick Ashton and *Theme and Variations* by George Balanchine. Despite the tremendous strain *Theme* put on his legs, Baryshnikov adapted to its style successfully. Owing to its lack of plot, *Theme* precluded any temptation to interpretation in the Stanislavskian key such as marked the dancer's classical roles. Ashton's *Les Patineurs* reminded Baryshnikov of Yakobson's ballet miniatures, but the latter's neoclassical patterns were invariably seasoned with a strong dash of histrionics. Ashton's choreography, elegantly designed in 1937, didn't contain any message other than the gaiety of a skating party. The part of the Green Skater, with his dazzling split *tour jeté*, the strings of low sautés and *ronds de jambe*, demanded merely neat, almost impersonal execution, though it placed Baryshnikov in the context of a kind of genre-painting scene. This ambience confused him at first by bringing out his Russian theatricality: the first time he performed the part he donned a red nose and very heavy makeup, with freckles, and made faces. His comments on *Les Patineurs* in *Baryshnikov at Work* are highly noteworthy: "After the first performance I abandoned all that, because the characterization is in the role, it's in the steps. You just don't need all that extra artificiality." This statement enunciated by a Soviet dancer, fostered in the traditions of Stanislavskian realism, sounds almost inconoclastic; it also demonstrates how swiftly Baryshnikov reevaluated his Russian approach. This process of change

th Maurice Béjart in Italy, 1975 / THOMAS VICTOR

continued throughout his "pre-Balanchine period" (1974–77), and each of his various roles stimulated it differently.

Le Jeune Homme et la Mort, the ballet that Antony Tudor suggested he try, gave Baryshnikov an opportunity to work with Roland Petit, of whom he had been fond since their brief meeting in Russia. There was another name hovering over *Le Jeune Homme*, whose attractiveness to Misha was as strong as Petit's—Jean Cocteau. He had seen his movies in Leningrad during the restricted shows for the so-called creative intelligentsia (they were never played for the public at

In Rome, 1975 / THOMAS VICTOR

large). *Orphée* was Misha's favorite. *Le Jeune Homme* harked back to the themes of *Orphée*—a poet's death; his continual resurrection by the creative process; death as a woman who loves the poet and guides him toward ultimate self-expression. In *Le Jeune Homme* these themes are blurred, because they have been transplanted to an obvious melodramatic ground. But the idea of death's temptation is there, as well as the image of a woman in a white dress with a train and long black gloves up to the elbow—Death as Maria Casarès played it in *Orphée*.

With a kind of childish abandon, Cocteau used to play with his favorite metaphysical motifs, placing them in a fairy-tale entourage (*La Belle et la Bête*) or in the whimsical decor of a historical legend (*L'Aigle à deux têtes*). Baryshnikov was attuned to the fact that *Le Jeune Homme* placed him in the context of the European culture he was eager to assimilate. For this particular reason he did not care that his young man—smoking in a cheap hotel room against the background of blinking electric signs, rebelling against the aggressive chaos of material things around him, and submitting himself to the power of the Death-woman—smacked of B-movie aesthetics in the 1970s.

The ballet, nurtured by Cocteau and Petit, was conceived in 1946 for the legendary Jean Babilée on the stage of Les Ballets des Champs-Elysées. In those days *Le Jeune Homme* reverberated in the neurotic atmosphere of postwar France, warming itself in the beams of Cocteau's glory as *enfant terrible*.

Partially due to his old feud with Cocteau, who unfairly ascribed the authorship of *Le Jeune Homme* as a ballet only to himself, Petit "brushed up" the ballet with an eye to Misha's personality. But its kinship to Cocteau's personal mythology took vengeance on Petit's new version. Here the delicate balance between poetry and camp, endemic to Cocteau's style, shifted heavily toward camp, resulting in a "copulation of clichés," as Nabokov would put it. They were somehow underscored by the solemn background of Bach's Passacaglia, maliciously substituted for jazz by Cocteau at the ballet's dress rehearsal in 1946. If in the earlier days Bach's music supported the Cocteau plot's leitmotifs of death and inspiration, now it simply put to shame the bare melodramatic intricacies.

Misha was aware of the clichés in this ballet and took a calculated risk for the sake of experiment. The choreography was truly unusual for him, with its sundry leaps, turns, acrobatic balances, and flights over the furniture. "You must run all over the stage, all over the furniture, all over the room, all over the ceiling practically by the time it's over," as he put it in *Baryshnikov at Work*. He loved the way the choreography was developing off the beat, or rather "the steps . . . arranged in groups that then must fit within a given time sequence." He was also thrilled with the existential motifs of the drama, which he had never had a chance to express in dance. For this particular reason, his experiment with Petit–Cocteau was not for him "a pathetic waste of his resources," as some critics maintained it was. Metaphysical content, or rather Baryshnikov's perception of drama in the metaphysical key, triggered some hidden emotional resources which he had once concealed in classical ballets. In *Le Jeune Homme* he led the audience to feel his very personal touch, possibly his own pent-up dissatisfaction or anger, which he had never displayed before. He had to let this petty demon out of the bottle to pursue the combat of "Baryshnikov against Baryshnikov" and win in the final analysis.

In Neumeier's *Hamlet Connotations* and Butler's *Medea*, both performed at ABT in January 1976, Misha seemed to be at a crossroads. The concrete qualities of the Shakespearean and mythological plots were effaced by the abstract language of the compositions. But the choreography was not sufficiently inventive in either case to break away from the plot and be transformed into the "choreographic poem" that Baryshnikov's body and burgeoning emotive resources would have written. He needed a ballet that would break radically with the classical dance and, more important, with the usual manner of presentation. He dreamed of a ballet in which the dance would exist only for the sake of the dance, without obvious references to his Russian classical baggage.

I recall a conversation we had in the winter of 1976, after *Medea*. I told him that Butler's trouble was in calling the ballet *Medea*. This immediately brings to mind specific cultural associations—we expect to see an interpretation of a theme, not formal, abstract movements that have no connection to *Medea* at all. The ballet would have gained a lot by remaining anonymous or taking a title like "Variations on the Medea Theme." Furthermore, Carla Fracci, with her superb romantic bearing, is no Medea.

Misha's response was surprising. "These ballets have helped me a lot, for all their imperfections; helped me to understand that, as much as I like narrative ballet, principal plot in ballet has outlived itself. The

eune Homme et la Mort / Martha Swope

alternatives are to do a dramatic ballet in the style of Yuri Grigorovich, or go the way of Balanchine, for whom plot is of no interest. And Balanchine is right—*Hamlet* is a play written in words, and as such it's great. Any of its adaptations in the language of another art are weaker than the original, and the performer is okay only if he's both an actor and a dancer. Ballet tends toward abstraction anyway. There's very little of *Anna Karenina* or *Hamlet* in the ballet versions other than melodrama, as we know from the Russian adaptations."

Baryshnikov's encounter with Twyla Tharp was timely. Her *Push Comes to Shove*, which premièred at ABT on January 9, 1976, was reminiscent of the Broadway musical, a lowly genre for the highbrow balletomane brought up on the aesthetics of Balanchine. But Balanchine might, after all, have prompted the approach of Twyla Tharp. In the opening of the *Donizetti Variations*, he slyly parodies the conventionality of the old classics, the preparation and the posing. The work demonstrates its genealogy, as it were, in order to take leave of it. But this is the buffoonery of a refined neoclassicist who truly knows his domain.

In *Push Comes to Shove*, Twyla Tharp was on unfamiliar ground. She is a dilettante in classical ballet and hardly capable of creating a convincing parody of it. Parody requires a mastery of the material that is being poked fun at. The easily recognized citations from classical ballets that abound in *Push* (including the Wilis' *arabesques voyagés* and the *danse des coupés* from *Swan Lake*) are nothing but well-known passages or shopworn clichés. But in Tharp's dilettantism is her strength. In my opinion, she is no "Bronislava Nijinska of our time," although the comparison has been made. Nijinska was a classicist to the marrow of her bones, and her experiments in *Les Noces* or *Les Biches* did not go any further than substitution of turned-in positions for turned-out ones or an expressive theatricality in the Fokine key. She was not a reformer of dance language; she was more of a stylist. In *Push*, Tharp showed herself to be a reformer who boldly turned away from tradition. *Push* draws the audience into a mildly cunning game in which the choreographer feigns being a simpleminded savage who looks on the classical contrivances with amazed, unbiased eyes. This game is a bit dangerous, because it can turn at any moment into an amateur hour. If there is a taunt in *Push*, it is Twyla's ironic attitude toward her own genealogy, which goes back to the extinct style of black dancers in blues performances.

Push Comes to Shove / MARTHA SWOPE

But it would seem that *Push* is about something else, and if there is in it, along with tomfoolery, a theme of sorts, then it is in the following: Tharp built the ballet on a symbiosis of American rag, Joseph Lamb's *Bohemia Rag* of 1919, and Haydn's 82nd Symphony. It was a risky fusion in principle, and one which was successful in the given case because all the elements were brought together in a deliberately popular style.

Casting aside the stylistic labels of music, Tharp constructed the ballet as a sort of dance continuum, as an apotheosis of the dancing body unconstrained by conceptions of a definite style. The choreography grows out of the "stylistic debris"; Tharp's talent is expressed in the infectiousness of this balletic bric-à-brac. Tharp doesn't parody the classical styles, not only because she does not know them sufficiently well, but also because that is easy. It is enough to disrupt the stylistic harmony in *Les Sylphides*, as it is performed at ABT or the Bolshoi, to have Fokine's aesthetic vignettes become parody and unambiguous camp (it's just possible that today they cannot be anything more than camp). *Push Comes to Shove* justifies its title in that it would only be a matter of sharpening it somewhat and the whole thing would move in the direction of the grotesque, something like the extravagances of the Ballet Trocadero de Monte Carlo. Tharp did, in fact, push it a bit too far; this resulted in an extreme style, whose charm is in its rhythmic flow, in its speed and devilishly refined combinations laced with brilliant gags. Here, the clichés of the classic movements are intentionally disjointed (a heel is pointed outward or downward, an arm moves in counterpoint, taut legs suddenly drag), or they are out of time with the music. Added to this are typically Tharpian shrugs, slouching, bumps, and contractions, the bedlam of rehearsal and the comic ritual of balletic curtain calls. However, this chaos of choreographic extremes is marvelously organized and the mix itself is natural and irresistible in its theatricality. This is no disservice to the classical dance, as some purists think—Tharp glorifies it in her own quite characteristic manner, bringing into being that synthesis of high and popular art that is typical of Balanchine. (It's another matter that with him the synthesis is achieved by nobler means.)

The ballet as fun, freed of its classical fetters—that was just what Baryshnikov needed in order to take one more important step on the path of realizing his resources. And Baryshnikov had not demonstrated the brilliant virtuosity in any work since *The Creation of the World* that he did in *Push*. Without him, this ballet is not alive, not only because no one else can so perfectly command all the balletic extremes which go to make up *Push*, but because Misha's great talent as a comic is essential to it. He showed the latter side of his art to America for the first time in *Push*; it was especially apparent in the improvisations. (Baryshnikov has a marvelous knack for mimicking styles of movement and conversational mannerisms, as his friends well know. Once, for the fun of it, he improvised impressions of Chaplin and other comedians from the silent films; he was hilarious.)

Twyla was the first to use his improvisational talents. Appearing on stage with two partners, Martine van Hamel and Marianna Tcherkassky, Misha wore a derby and a campy outfit. He went through his whole incredible bag of tricks in the form of an improvisation, though every movement had been calculated almost mathematically. The improvisational feeling was underscored by the first solo. After a cascade of jitterbugging, pelvis-thumping, loose-limbed movements, he seemed to switch off, walking around in circles, running his fingers through his hair, getting ready to go into the next cascade. The uniqueness of *Push*, as Arlene Croce noted, is in the fact that "the dancing gives us more of Baryshnikov, the twentieth-century, 'American Baryshnikov,' than anything else he has done so far, and the 'rests' give us more of him, too—more than we normally see in the walking and posing that come between the step sequences in a classical ballet. His personality does not go behind a cloud, as it often does when he isn't dancing; it continues to radiate."

After the strenuous yet gratifying experiment with Twyla Tharp, Baryshnikov ventured into new territory by taking part in the movie *The Turning Point*, directed by Herbert Ross. This undertaking was also laborious, but less pleasing.

The screenplay by Arthur Laurents, with its soap-opera flavor, sought to develop a rather trite story about the relationship between two ballerinas—Emma (Anne Bancroft) and Deedee (Shirley MacLaine). Misha, who admires Visconti, Bergman, Fellini, Chaplin, and Buñuel, was not overly impressed.

His supporting role as Yuri Kopeikin, "the Russian maverick from the moon" (the story doesn't make clear how he got to the West), was meant to capitalize on the superficial Baryshnikov image fabricated by the mass media: a playboy, changing women like gloves, reveling in his

With Goulue and Katia in his New York apartment / PHOTO © BY LEONID LUBIANITSK

irresistibility and malicious charm. This image had as much bearing to Baryshnikov as a person as the whole movie did to the real problems of the contemporary ballet world. Instead, the film concentrated on the domestic climate of American Ballet Theatre, with which Herbert Ross and his "right hand," Nora Kaye, one of the greatest American ballerinas of the past, had long been affiliated. The ABT company served as the fictionalized backdrop of the film's setting.

The movie was alluring to cognoscenti, who were thrilled when they recognized ABT's familiar hectic everyday life, its tiffs and intrigues, little joys and griefs, as well as a Lucia Chase substitute. For the public at large it was a modest yet, unfortunately, unimaginative introduction to ballet cuisine.

Baryshnikov's Yuri was relegated to the periphery of the film, forced to pick up the few dramatic crumbs left by Bancroft and MacLaine. But if *The Turning Point* did not add more luster to their fame, Baryshnikov's participation contributed greatly to the balletic glory of the movie.

The film was released in November 1977, and Baryshnikov's art put to shame the legendary circling *chaînés* of Vakhtang Chabukiani in the film version of *La Bayadère*. Even Nureyev's feline jumps in the filmed pas de deux from *Le Corsaire* paled in comparison to Baryshnikov's almost inconceivable purity, displayed in his *sauts de basque* or grand pirouettes. It was almost frightening to see the academic principles enunciated so fully on the screen, without any visible effort. Baryshnikov's dancing constituted the major value of the movie, making up for the anemic qualities of his part.

His English in 1976 was far from being pronounced "trippingly on the tongue," and as a result, his screen image disappointed him. Also, he was annoyed by the fact that a movie actor is forced to function under total control of a director, who in the process of editing is entitled to twist the celluloid image in any possible way. Television seemed to offer more exciting possibilities: there one could check every shot by redoing it in accordance with one's own aesthetic standards. Essentially, Misha's dislike for the movies derived from his frustrated desire to express his real personality. When asked to play a leading role in Herbert Ross's *Nijinsky*, he rejected the part, disregarding the fat fee. He turned down many other screenplays written for him after his success in *The Turning Point*, even after the encouragement of an Academy Award nomination in the category of best supporting actor. One hopes his disillusionment is temporary. At the very least his performance in *The Turning Point* accelerated the expansion of the ballet's audience—a trend initiated in the West by Rudolf Nureyev. Nureyev's magnetic personality widened the limited circle of ballet-goers, doing for ballet the very thing that Maria Callas had done for opera. As a result of his electrifying personality on stage, Nureyev's image was equated to that of a movie star rather than that of a pure dance performer. Baryshnikov followed the path cleared by Nureyev. By conquering mass audiences, classical ballet is turning into another form of escapism. In an unstable world, classical ballet demonstrates the triumph of order over chaos. It provides an illusion of stability, which is in itself soothing and enticing. And Baryshnikov's image alone is the most beautiful form of stability.

Misha's image was not totally misrepresented by the film, despite its emphasis on his seductively winsome qualities. His comments on ballet as a conscientious job, a serious duty to which he is committed, helped to shatter the persistent myth about ballet as an undignified profession for young men. And in *The Turning Point* Misha certainly revealed more of his true personality than do the flashier periodicals. He is not a flippant "*coureur*," a habitué of discotheques, hanging around the glittering company of movie stars and the jet set. Baryshnikov's social life is not hectic. His private world is strictly confined to his classes, rehearsals, performances, and his books, country house, and few close friends. He prefers the company of Joseph Brodsky, the Russian poet, to any fancy party. His reputation as a playboy is also a creation of the media. By nature he is neither more nor less fickle than most of his contemporaries. His romance of three years with the movie actress Jessica Lange is nurtured by mutual affection and respect. In a good sense, Misha is old-fashioned and protective of his integrity. He is sensitive to any kind of phoniness—his shyness and reserve are in part restraint against curtly dismissing pretension with an ironic response.

When commissioned to interview Baryshnikov for the TV program *60 Minutes*, Mike Wallace, who had never met Misha, asked me for advice regarding the best way to approach him. "Try to be as casual and simple with him as possible," I said. "He is not hard to communicate with if you don't involve him in a social game. Once he senses gamesmanship in his interlocutor, he dismisses conversation with a joke, taking advantage of his natural charm and sense of humor. He will place you against his radiant façade and you'll never be able to

With Goulue on the terrace of his New York apartment / PHOTO © BY
LEONID LUBIANITSKY

Le Spectre de la Rose, with Marianna Tcherkassky / MARTHA SWOPE

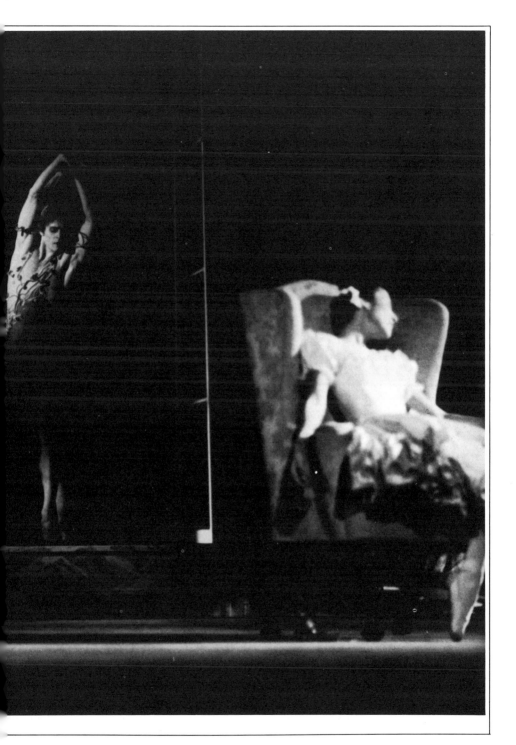

Le Spectre de la Rose, with Marianna Tcherkassky / MARTHA SWOPE

penetrate it. The way birds know their own language, responding to particular notes, his 'human substance' reacts only to the notes of seriousness or spontaneity. If you hit the right notes, he will pour forth his feelings in the most surprising way. He dislikes interviews, because he is constantly expected to mouth something sensational, referring to his stardom. It sickens him. And don't ask him about his private life. That's like his country house, a forbidden ground where 'unauthorized personnel are not admitted.' "

By tackling the American Ballet Theatre's productions of *Le Spectre de la Rose* and *Petrouchka*, Baryshnikov intruded on Nijinsky's illustrious domain. What is more, both parts, created by Fokine as distinctive dance therapy for Nijinsky's tormented genius, aroused Baryshnikov's interest in the mysterious personality of the legendary dancer. Oddly enough, the part of the Spectre, regarded in the history of ballet as the most flamboyant example of Nijinsky's virtuosity, provided too poor a vehicle for Baryshnikov to fully demonstrate his artistry. Fokine's choreography seemed to service only two of the chief virtues of Nijinsky's dance personality: his *ballon*, or the ability to sustain a jump in the air, and the androgyny that was implied by Fokine's choreographic patterns, justifying the substitution of a rose for a man. Neither element was Baryshnikov's forte.

Le Spectre is a technical tour de force, shaped as an unabated stream of *sissonnes*, alternating with *entrechats six*, coming from and to a closed fifth position. In Fokine's time it was considered the pinnacle of male technical virtuosity. To cope with it as effortlessly as Nijinsky, by all accounts, did, one has to possess his rare ankle muscle endurance, as well as the ability to take off cleanly after being so strained.

Baryshnikov was conscious of being miscast, but that challenged him. As he put it, in *Baryshnikov at Work*, "I don't have a naturally short take-off, this kind of continual plié into big jumps makes it virtually impossible for me to get through the role . . ." In Russia in the sixties only Yuri Soloviev, endowed with his fabulous *ballon*, presented a perfect replica of Nijinsky's Spectre, visually reincarnating that "victorious attack of rose perfume" that Nijinsky's image, according to Jean Cocteau, allegorized. In comparison with Soloviev's, Baryshnikov's Spectre was less striking technically and far more refined. He saturated the strings of impetuous movements with his unique fluidity, which made the strain on his legs almost invisible. He by no means recalled a dancing androgynous creature whose mysterious sex appeal had once so devastatingly reverberated in Paris, "submerged in the erotic twilight," as Marcel Proust noted. Baryshnikov's infectiousness derived from a subtle sexual ambivalence, generated by a slightly effeminate plasticity, which he skillfully mimicked. By muting the ostentatious sexual emphasis, Baryshnikov modernized Fokine's concept.

As for *Petrouchka*: the work on this part induced him to write the most illuminating chapter in *Baryshnikov at Work*. His speculations on Petrouchka were strongly influenced by Vera Krassovskaya's book on Nijinsky. In creating Petrouchka for Nijinsky, Fokine aimed at achieving a kind of malicious psychoanalysis through his dancing. Outwardly the role was designed with an eye to Nijinsky's bizarre behavior in life—his mechanical gestures, wooden manner, strikingly unprepossessing face (akin to Buster Keaton's stone face). What is more, the similarity between Petrouchka's relationship with the Old Magician and that of Nijinsky and Diaghilev was meant to put the dancer's complex inner mechanism into motion. His suppressed resentment, self-pity—all the facets of a "trapped soul"—were to surface in order to stun the audience with the force of pain.

Fokine's experiment was more than successful: according to Fedor Lopukhov, Nijinsky's classmate. Petrouchka not only miraculously mirrored the most salient traits of his character but added a tragic dimension to it. (Benois even believed that, owing to his identification with Petrouchka, Nijinsky was able to escape from Diaghilev's gentle captivity.) Without the piercing emotional outpouring, spontaneously addressed to the audience, Petrouchka is as dead as a cartoon buffoon. No wonder the attempts of Nureyev and Erik Bruhn to bring Petrouchka to life through pure theatricality were disappointing.

One statement in Baryshnikov's chapter on *Petrouchka* is especially notable: "The characterization is extremely clear, but difficult to make natural. The use of a puppetlike style must, first of all, be clearly designed and then performed with a seamless, fluid ease so that it becomes its own standard, so that the audience doesn't feel that the dancer is 'playing a doll.' " With his peaked, mobile features, distant eyes, and flexible body, Baryshnikov was simply born for the part, but his first performances were uneven. Petrouchka as a character eluded Baryshnikov: he was playing a doll. The real miracle happened during

ouchka / MARTHA SWOPE

a performance in the summer of 1977 at the Met, when out of the conventional mask of an underdog from Russian folklore the suffering face of a child suddenly peered. His plasticity took on the character of Chaplinesque angularity and vulnerable awkwardness, and the wealth of emotional colors his body unearthed—all the mercurial transitions from joy to resentment, humiliation to triumph—were breathtaking. It was as if an old painting, familiar but dim, had been cleaned to its original tints.

It is tempting to try to guess what particular feelings guided Baryshnikov in his piercing characterization. When I asked him, he seemed to be at a loss. Possibly, they are the same feelings that feed his affection for animals or, in a broader sense, his sympathy with all kinds of clown-underdogs; dancers, after all, are almost as dependent on the will of a choreographer as Petrouchka is on the Old Magician's whims. Perhaps his empathy went deeper, encompassing the problem of freedom in general.

As Petrouchka, Baryshnikov added to his genuine comic gift a tragic dimension, which, in my view, constitutes the major facet of his personality. So far, as a rare example of self-revelation, his Petrouchka is unequaled in the gallery of Baryshnikov's ballet portrayals. Only in the part of Hermann in the one-act ballet *The Queen of Spades* by Roland Petit did he continue this process of self-revelation.

At the outset, it was intended that *The Queen of Spades* would be performed to Prokofiev's music, which he had written for film and radio presentations, but which was preserved only in the archives. (For some inexplicable reason, most likely due to the criminal neglect of Russian culture by the powers that be, the score has never been published.) Unfortunately, the Party purveyors of red tape had banned the work, and so it turned out to be unavailable to Petit. It is possible that if the neglected Prokofiev had fallen into his hands, the score would have pushed the ballet master toward bold dance resolutions.

Petit turned to the opera music of Tchaikovsky, which lent itself poorly to reworking as a series of ballet numbers. Tchaikovsky, it seems to me, transformed Petit's fantasy into a more traditional dramatic ballet. Moreover, in adapting the opera score for the ballet, Petit and his arranger emphasized the dance quality of the work, disregarding its major philosophical leitmotifs. As a result, certain musical nonsense arose: the appearance of the Old Countess coincides with Pauline's romance from the opera's second act; Hermann and Liza's first duet is performed in the style of an old minuet to the music of the pastorale from the third act, which is purely a divertissement, bearing no relation to Hermann's drama. It's no wonder that these liberties evoked the censure of the Tchaikovsky specialists.

The absence in the ballet score of the major leitmotifs of fore-doomed love and inevitable death somehow turned Tchaikovsky's most Wagnerian opera, his "drama of fate," into the psychological drama of Hermann. In Pushkin's tale and in Tchaikovsky's music, the drama of the poor young officer, Hermann, is that his faith in the magic secret of three cards, which the old Countess, according to drawing-room anecdote, possesses, grows into an obsession with winning. This maniacal obsession destroys Hermann's love for Liza and drives him mad; he is lost between fancy and reality. (No wonder Dostoevsky was very fond of this Pushkin hero.) Fate, in the form of a playing card, the queen of spades, which in Hermann's inflamed mind is associated with the old Countess, punishes him for the obsessive idea that killed the man in him. The ideological polyphony of the tale and the opera was tossed overboard in the ballet, not only because including it in the framework of a one-act performance would be almost impossible. Petit consciously simplified his problem, creating a minia-ture Petersburg drama with Hermann as hero, a passionate gambler.

In its favor, the ballet is a monodrama for Baryshnikov that utilizes him well as a dancer and as a tragic actor. Its weakness is that Petit accented the secondary themes of *The Queen of Spades*—the city and the little man of dark passions, an underground man more in the Dos-toevskian mold than in that of the mystical romanticism of Pushkin.

The sparse design of André Beaurepaire gave a Petersburg tonality to the events. Two forward wings are furnished with gray Greek columns wound with black ribbons, suggesting the pseudo-classical architecture of Petersburg. These columns, which do not support any-thing, rise in exaggerated perspective on the single, painted backdrop and are rather reminiscent of the colonnades in the surrealistic paint-ings of Delvaux and de Chirico. Playing cards caught by the wind hang between them. This is the image of the Petersburg of Dostoevsky, a city where reality is transformed into dream or a trick of the imagina-tion. Everyday details indicating the place of action (the table in the gaming house, a chair, screen, and mirror in the Countess's bedroom) appear against the backdrop, which is as gray as the Petersburg sky.

The figure of Hermann—Baryshnikov clad in an officer's uniform

The Queen of Spades / SETH EASTMAN
MOEBS; (ABOVE) PHOTO LAVOLÉ

—emerges from the depths of the stage and makes its way from one circle of street-lamp light to another, on the way to the gaming house. The first monologue, with its headlong, ragged movements and mechanical gestures, is an exposition of character. Baryshnikov highlights the image of a frenzied young man obsessed with card playing.

The gaming house, in Petit, is not the gay refuge of Hussar officers, with its champagne and pert Gypsy beauties, that it is in Pushkin. It is seen, rather, in terms of the famous gamblers of Baudelaire. The dancers, as gamblers, have the acquired mechanical movements of marionettes and are directed by a banker with an immobile chalk-white face. The gamblers take a card and cover their hand with their palm, making way for a new group of players. Here, no one loses or wins. This is unmotivated action that has no end—a game in its pure form, momentary gratification.

Petit was quite right to make the old Countess, not Liza, the heroine of the ballet, putting Jacqueline Rayet on pointes for the role. Hermann's love for Liza in this drama is a passion corrupted by the

The Queen of Spades / SETH EASTMAN MOEBS

passion for winning: Liza is the means to obtain the Countess's fabled secret of the three cards.

Petit's choreography combined two distinct styles: the intentionally expressionistic, conveying Hermann's insanity, and the static, meant to demonstrate his returns to a normal state of mind. Reveling in both, Baryshnikov made much use of his virtuosity and dramatic impact to create an utterly neurotic character in the grip of his mood fluctuations. Thus the gallant minuet with Liza, whom Hermann almost cynically seduced to snatch the key from the old Countess's bedroom, precipitously turns into a cascade of alternating air turns and jumps. The mime conversation with the old Countess at the ball, where Hermann pleads with her to divulge the secret of the three cards, is suddenly interrupted by Hermann's whirlwind solo, at the end of which, as if coming out of another unpredictable fit, he freezes on demi-pointes at the footlights, then flees, covering his face with his hands.

The juxtaposition of the two styles comes to a climax in the crucial episode, which takes place in the old Countess's bedroom. In his tempestuous solo, saturated with energetic persistence, Hermann-Baryshnikov stretches his body into a line, as if diving into water, covering the whole stage with one soaring jump, to fall prone upon the old Countess's feet, frightening her to death. (The same breathtaking jump was repeated in the barracks scene, when, in an attempt to catch up with the evanescent ghost of the old Countess, he lands in the emptiness of the spotlight.) The fit of delirium alternates again with a state bordering on apathy: Hermann lingers over the old Countess's dead body, vaguely staring at some distant point in the audience.

The last game, in which his life is at stake, was structured as a pure mime. Hermann flies out of the wings, turning his back to the audience and changing direction in the flash of a second to find himself in front of the green table. As if in his last duel with destiny, Hermann-Baryshnikov collects all his strength to tame insanity. He takes the first imaginary card, quietly raising the empty hand to show his triumph. He opens the second one after a pause, facing the table and enjoying the bewilderment of the gamblers. The third he clasps to his breast, without opening it, feverishly savoring his supreme victory. Hermann's rival reveals his card first, with an authoritarian gesture, as if saying: "Your queen of spades is covered . . ."

Unfortunately, Petit could not find an effective theatrical device to make clear how Hermann penetrated the ill-fated secret of the three cards. The three ballerinas disguised as the doubles of the old Countess, displaying pictures of the cards, resemble a quotation from a Soviet drama ballet. Nevertheless, Baryshnikov's tragic intensity helped to fill this gap in the consistency of the ballet plot.

In *The Queen of Spades* Baryshnikov portrayed a complex, neurotic character for the first time. His talent for tragedy, revealed in *Petrouchka*, also manifested itself in Petit's plot ballet. His long affair with dramatic storytelling ballets was not yet finished.

Baryshnikov's sense of drama became even more apparent in his approach to the classical legacy by way of his own versions of *The Nutcracker* and *Don Quixote*. He revised these classics for the American Ballet Theatre, and they premièred in December 1977 and March 1978 respectively.

7 CHOREOGRAPHIC DEBUTS

◁ Rehearsal for the television production of *The Nutcracker* / MARTHA SWOPE

DANCE CRITIC Arlene Croce glimpsed in Baryshnikov's choreography for *The Nutcracker* the usual Soviet interpretation of Tchaikovsky's ballet. She was apparently referring to the attempt to read the music philosophically, thanks to which *The Nutcracker* was transformed into a "ballet for adults." This was far from the spectacle of the imperial theater that Tchaikovsky and Petipa, the librettist, and Ivan Vsevolojsky, the artistic supervisor at Leningrad's Maryinsky, were originally aiming for. Moreover, in the subtext of her review, Croce seemed to underscore the "priority" of Balanchine's version, which, it is generally thought, reproduces the general features of the original ballet by Petipa and Ivanov. This "authenticity" in Balanchine's production is frequently proclaimed as a guarantee of its artistic qualities.

But *The Nutcracker* is a special case, since the Petipa-Ivanov production (which was basically Ivanov's, under the aegis of Petipa) was hardly irreproachable. The ballet's four creators—Vsevolojsky, Tchaikovsky, Petipa, and Ivanov—had some mutually exclusive views about Hoffmann's fairy tale of the little girl, Clara (in the Russian version, Masha), who fell in love with a freakish-looking toy. Vsevolojsky wanted to treat the tsarist court to dances in the spirit of Parisian *ballets féeriques*. Tchaikovsky wrote a serious symphonic composition, whose non-canonical quality evoked the angry indignation of the ballet critics. Ivanov's gifts were not up to coping with music imbued with Hoffmannesque imagery. Meanwhile, Petipa, who was sick and already past eighty, did nothing but issue instructions to follow the style of Vsevolojsky, which was sometimes inconsistent with the music, often at cross-purposes to it. It is not surprising that the production was criticized from the day of its creation. It was removed from the repertoire many times, and in 1922 it was redone completely, so that even Ivanov's choreography was lost. This fact speaks for itself—nothing of the kind happened with *Swan Lake* or *The Sleeping Beauty* or *La Bayadère*; no matter how they were patched together, the basis of the choreography remained unchanged. It is no wonder that Balanchine's version, which he reproduced from his earliest recollections (he danced the Nutcracker prince and jester in the second decade of this century), preserves the old weaknesses, though the final pas de deux reveals the hand of Balanchine himself, whose signature is clearly distinct from Ivanov's. The music's tragic sense is still untouched by the rosy fairy tale. It's curious that the best part in Balanchine's

Nutcracker is the same as, by all accounts, it was in Ivanov's—the dance of the snowflakes. Then, too, the general atmosphere of the Christmas tale, more in the manner of Dickens than Hoffmann, is successful.

Baryshnikov, who knew the sad history of *The Nutcracker*, did not undertake any sort of restoration. In working on the ballet, Baryshnikov used me as a sort of artistic consultant. We discussed the libretto in detail and its old disharmony with the music, and attempted to adjust one to the other. In the course of our research, we came upon Petipa's newly published elaboration of *The Nutcracker* and Fedor Lopukhov's commentary. Lopukhov was a talented choreographer in the twenties, the first to rework Ivanov's production. We were both struck by the fact that apparently Petipa himself had felt the incompatibility of the music and the libretto and had conceived the second act not at all as the gala divertimento in Confitürenburg that emerged subsequently. He had in mind a "harmonious refuge" that would have had something in common with Robespierre's dream of the harmony of society and nature—the so-called holiday of "the Supreme Being." Petipa would have finished, oddly enough, with a French Revolutionary dance, a carmagnole. His last words in the libretto are noteworthy: "Off on the good path, dear du Mille" (from a children's song referring to Charles X's flight to England).

How Petipa connected the French Revolution and *The Nutcracker* is difficult to say—perhaps through some personal myth from his childhood, which was spent in Marseilles, home of "La Marseillaise." Nevertheless, Petipa stands at the source of serious interpretations of the score of *The Nutcracker*. It is possible that in order not to anger his influential patron, Vsevolojsky, Petipa consciously avoided fullfledged involvement in the ballet's production. His ideas contained too much from the carmagnole for the stagnant imperial stage. If so, it was not simply the illness and feebleness of the maestro that led him to dump an excessive burden onto the fragile shoulders of Ivanov—a master of elegant miniatures but not of full-length ballets.

In an effort to remove some of the original disparity between music and subject in *The Nutcracker*, Baryshnikov followed Petipa and other choreographers—Lopukhov and Vainonen of the twenties and thirties; Grigorovich and Tchernichov of the sixties. Among them, he sought a happy balance. As Baryshnikov put it in an interview to be broadcast to Russia by the Voice of America: "*The Nutcracker* was more of an experiment as a director for me. I paid tribute in it to my predecessors; the interpretation was mine. The very idea of the construction of a ballet interested me. I didn't even consider absolutely new choreography for this music, undoubtedly the most complicated in ballet."

Baryshnikov, the director, followed Tchaikovsky and Hoffmann. He endowed Drosselmeyer with the features of a Hoffmann magician who goes from being Clara's godfather to her tempter, hastening, as it were, her ripening. At first he conceived of him as a romantic poet composing a Christmas tale for Clara and the audience. He would push back the curtain to present the entire ballet as the fruit of his indefatigable imagination and to participate in it rightfully as Clara's godfather, using the somewhat grotesque toy nutcracker to "test" the girl. And only when she had fallen in love with the freakish toy did he turn it into a prince, leaving Clara in a fairy-tale world and closing the curtain before the spectators.

However, this conception subsequently seemed too daring in relation to the tradition. Therefore, Drosselmeyer became a Hoffmann miracle worker instead of a romantic poet, but the idea of a "theater within a theater" remained. The ballet opens with a short prologue in Drosselmeyer's workshop, where he has created the dolls that he rehearses for Clara's fairy tale. At the height of the Christmas holiday, he presents his doll spectacle to Clara and her friends in order to prepare her for the miracles of Christmas night—a night for testing her humanity and for bidding farewell to childhood. The theme of disenchantment, of parting with illusions, is quite close to Baryshnikov himself. He is by nature a disillusionist who is not at all inclined to be diverted by the unrealizable and who seriously weighs reality's choices.

To create the miracles on stage in the first act is particularly difficult. It is necessary to justify the romantic transition from reality to fancy (Clara's so-called dream) and to make accessible to the audience that almost imperceptible watershed that separates them in Hoffmann, who does not delineate the two distinctly in the story. Fantasy encroaches on reality, magically transforming it and creating that romantic disorder which is the spirit of Hoffmanniana.

Therefore, Baryshnikov moved the transformation of Drosselmeyer's dolls to the first act—Harlequin, Columbine, and the Moor come to life with a magical wave of his black silk cape. The variations of each of the three are original and do not recall Baryshnikov's predecessors. The night scene, where Clara sneaks up to the tree in her nightdress in order to be alone with her beloved oddity, is thus foreshadowed. Baryshnikov's construction of the scene is most convincing.

Clara nestles down with her darling, only to be roused a moment later by the onslaught of the mice from the doll spectacle, dressed in the manner of her parents' guests: the carelessness and aggressiveness of adults was emphasized earlier in the episode when a tipsy guest tore off the freakish Nutcracker's head. Therefore, in her dream, the pushy and funny mice from Drosselmeyer's doll show and the overwhelming guests at the Christmas party merge in Clara's consciousness. Mice in the guests' images had already appeared in Lopukhov's and Tchernichov's versions, but this derivation did not bother Baryshnikov. They created a special theatrical effect that was redoubled in the "single combat with the Mouse King."

Whether the onslaught of the mice is a dream or not is not entirely clear in Baryshnikov's staging. And this constitutes a Hoffmannesque and romantic understatement that obliterates the distinction between reality and fancy. In order to set off the romantic nature of the understatement, Drosselmeyer is introduced in the capacity of maker of events—a demiurge.

Against the background of the Christmas tree, which grows in response to Drosselmeyer's design, the Nutcracker is transformed and acquires human dimensions. The scene of his duel with the Mouse King is the most original part of the first act. Here, the Nutcracker's virtuoso variation on a hobby horse, the skirmish of the two armies, and the sword fight between the Nutcracker and the puffed-up Mouse King (the comic treatment of whom is more than appropriate) are successful. The entire scene of the battle is sustained in a humorous vein. (The defeated King is carried out by his subjects, his body slung from their hands as if he were a stuck hog.) The tone recalls for the viewer that this dream—or fantastic reality—exists through the efforts of Drosselmeyer, whose ironic gaze belies the look of an adult who is arranging a bit of fun for Clara.

When Drosselmeyer transforms the Nutcracker-freak into a prince, the tone of the choreographic tale changes—now the point of view of Clara, who finally meets her dream, is introduced. The Prince is a reward for her humanity, thanks to which she loved a freak, so to speak. Baryshnikov intentionally deprived the Prince-Nutcracker of characteristic features. He is faceless and conditional, as appropriate to an "ideal" fairy-tale prince dwelling in childish consciousness. He is merely an instrument in the hands of Drosselmeyer, who makes his goddaughter a gift of her dream in the flesh in order to take it away in the second act, as if to say: "That's it, my dear, get used to the fact that in life there is no place for dreams."

The Nutcracker and Clara's adagio is an original composition—a prelude to their "through-the-looking-glass journey" through the winter forest, where snowmaidens, again according to the will of the all-powerful magician Drosselmeyer, perform their circle dances. Baryshnikov kept the snowmaidens from Vasily Vainonen's version, out of respect for this Russian exemplar of noble academicism. I feel that this was a mistake. Unexpectedly, the choreographer's relationship to the action, which is now ironic through Drosselmeyer's eyes, now lyric through Clara's, disappears here. Vainonen's rendition looks too academic, too neutral, and the effect is lost. Here, by the logic of Baryshnikov's version, there ought to have been a definite emotional coloration. The greatest accomplishment of Baryshnikov the choreographer—rather, the director—is his provision of a logical basis for the wide variety of divertissements. These numbers are justified as the dances of courtiers in honor of Clara, the Nutcracker's deliverer.

Baryshnikov also made inroads into the notorious problems with the so-called farewell adagio for Clara and the Prince. Tchaikovsky's music in *The Nutcracker* attains a maximum of tragic intensity in this scene and has been a stumbling block for the whole generation of Russian choreographers from Ivanov to Vainonen and Grigorovich. The plaintive, requiem-like qualities of the music (which was composed in memory of Tchaikovsky's dead sister) used to be somewhat compromised by a trivial adagio of a ballerina with a partner or four cavaliers. Thus it was in Vainonen's version; thus it basically remained in Grigorovich's awkward attempt to adapt this highly un-Mendelssohnian music to Clara and the Prince's wedding needs.

In the context of the plot Baryshnikov carefully set out, Tchaikovsky's heartrending piece conveys a quite appropriate meaning: Drosselmeyer's fairy tale is over, and he, as purveyor of this elusive Christmas dream for his goddaughter, interferes to destroy its magic and return Clara to reality. (Incidentally, the same device was employed by Igor Tchernichov in his innovative production of *The Nutcracker* in Odessa, in 1970, which Baryshnikov never had a chance to see.)

Instead of the traditional adagio, Baryshnikov introduced a trio, structured as a struggle between Drosselmeyer and the Prince for Clara. It is assessed by Baryshnikov as the combat of a girl's enduring dream and the dream-maker's will to give a cruel lesson to his godchild. As for the trio's choreography, it could have been far more inventive and less academic; in particular, the promenade of both competitors around Clara, frozen in arabesque, is too obviously related to the "Rose Adagio" from *The Sleeping Beauty*. In this trio, Baryshnikov wrongly confined himself within strictly classical patterns. The music demands some neoclassical compositions, more daring, actively disrupting the traditional approach. But in terms of stage direction the trio is one of the most dramatic pieces in the production, rivaled only by Clara's odd vision, the sort of surrealistic nightmare, preceding the finale. This delirium, provoked by Drosselmeyer, is composed of the odds and ends persisting in Clara's imagination: the marching toy soldiers, the lost doll, Harlequin, one snowflake lagging behind the rest.

Final *pas de trois* from *The Nutcracker*, with Natalia Makarova and Alexander Min?
DINA MAKAROVA

Among them the Prince Charming and Clara's illusions are lost forever. This whimsical bric-à-brac disappears at the behest of Drosselmeyer, completing his pedagogic experiment to strengthen Clara to face her new day. In the finale of the ballet this idea is visibly brought about: the morning light that infiltrates the imaginary window is a metaphor for maturity, the inner strength with which Drosselmeyer endows the sensitive girl.

In his interpretation, Baryshnikov was only mildly concerned with the Freudian implications coloring the Drosselmeyer-Clara relationship. And if his *Nutcracker* has a message, it should be read as a moral approach to character, which, by all accounts, had also inspired Tchaikovsky in composing his musical score. In this respect, Baryshnikov's choreographic transcription of *The Nutcracker* seems to me the closest to its composer's intentions.

When Baryshnikov turned to *Don Quixote*, it was as a continuation of his "experiments as a director," this time using the material from what is probably Petipa's most amusing ballet. The work grew out of one episode from Cervantes's philosophical novel—the wedding of the barber Basilio to the village beauty Quiteria. The novel has only the most distant relationship to all balletic transcriptions of it by Noverre, Milon, Didelot, and Petipa. Only through some unfortunate misunderstanding does the immortal knight of the woeful countenance figure in the title of the ballet. Don Quixote is hardly connected at all with the marriage of the obstinate Kitri and the cunning Basil. The lines are tangled, in the manner of vaudeville, but this comic marriage intrigue with its inevitable happy ending is a genre that was very popular in the Russian theater of the nineteenth century.

Baryshnikov did not attempt any sort of restoration; a remake of Petipa's production would be impossible. The old maestro himself redid it twice, creating one version for Moscow, another for Petersburg, where the richness of the dance was undermined by a dearth of theatrical devices and the weakness of dramaturgy. In 1900, a disciple of Petipa's, Alexander Gorsky, "re-edited" *Don Quixote*, bringing it close to a Spanish show for the consumption of Moscovite aficionados of spectacle. He revised it to such a degree that Soviet versions of the ballet began to rely more heavily on the Petipa elements. (In America, people basically know Petipa-Gorsky's Bolshoi version with Maya Plisetskaya as an incomparable Kitri.)

Don Quixote rehearsal / BLIOKH ▷

Don Quixote rehearsal / BLIOKH

Baryshnikov had a free hand with *Don Quixote*. As compared to *The Nutcracker*, its tradition was much less binding; then, too, Minkus's music is operatic, the antithesis of symphonic, and permits variations this way and that. Therefore, the critical voices heard after the première at the Kennedy Center in Washington in the spring of 1977 were quite beside the point in maintaining that the Bolshoi version was closer to the original and so, a priori, better, and that Baryshnikov had "Americanized" the Petipa-Gorsky work almost in the tradition of a Broadway show. An authentic *Don Quixote* does not exist. It is sufficient to look at the history of the final pas de deux, which Baryshnikov performed brilliantly with Gelsey Kirkland or Natalia Makarova, to understand this.

As a sort of circus act or balletic *morceau de virtuosité*, the piece has been around for almost a hundred years. In Petipa's first version, this duet was not included at all; in the second version it was an incidental number, with a classical dancer extraneous to the action as Kitri's partner rather than Basil. It was a sheer divertissement. Only Gorsky put Basil in at this point, crowning the ballet with an effective number that is supposed to demonstrate the triumph of love. In the thirties, this piece was laced with all the achievements of the male dance in Soviet ballet. Alexei Yermolaev and Vakhtang Chabukiani stuffed into it all the tricks they knew. In their footsteps, Boris Bregvadze and Valery Panov at the Kirov, and especially Vladimir Vasiliev at the Bolshoi, dressed up the pas de deux, each in his own way, and gave new life to a threadbare balletic display. Petipa created his ballet as a tribute to his youthful love affair with Spain, where, as a carefree rake, he had experienced wild romantic adventures, one ending in a duel. It was one of his first experiments in combining the classics with character dance, in which the mass of the corps de ballet and the soloists' numbers held equal sway. This nineteenth-century novelty would not have saved the ballet from oblivion, and it might well have died, as did Petipa's *Pharaoh's Daughter* or *Le Roi Candaule*, were it not for the obsession of the Soviet ballet of the thirties with heroes of the simple folk as opposed to rich dunderheads. The related theme was "the people are the moving force of history," and Cervantes was canonized in the Soviet Union as the bard of poor Spain and its unfortunate masses.

Baryshnikov had all this in mind when he took up *Don Quixote*, and he had no thought of any sort of "Americanization." His point of departure was the overall classical experience of Petipa and Gorsky's theatricality, but he decided to render the balletic history of the work in a manner quite correct for the 1970s. The ironic approach to his youthful interpretation of Basil was carried over into the entire ballet. Pointedly calling the work *Don Quixote or the Wedding of Basil and Kitri*, Baryshnikov was giving Petipa his due, as it were. (The initial announcements of his ballet contained both titles joined by "or.") On the other hand, he selected the tried-and-true form of "ballet vaudeville," which he worked out in the manner of Gorsky.

The most difficult thing was to justify the presence of Don Quixote in the ballet. The old versions, particularly the Kirov, presented a rather tedious prologue in which the crazy old man digs in some dusty volumes, nurturing his dream of Dulcinea. His Sancho runs in, escaping from some peasants from whom he had stolen a ham, before setting out with his cranky master in search of the beautiful lady. Baryshnikov quite correctly cut out all of this antediluvian nonsense as an explanation of Don Quixote's appearance in the action. Instead, to the overture, in which musical, albeit primitive, characterizations are given, he set forth a prologue in a light, ironic tone. The heroes run out on stage in the manner of the Italian *commedia dell'arte* (with which the Russian vaudeville is intimately related through French comedy), and they freeze in characteristic poses. Amour pierces Don Quixote with an arrow; the heroes, each in his own way, grab their hearts in an intentionally theatrical manner. A comic tone is given to the action, and it continues through the entire production. Of course, the logic of a vaudeville *Don Quixote* is weak and shouldn't be judged by the criteria of serious dramaturgy. But at least the work is relieved of absurdity. This was Baryshnikov's goal.

Moreover, Petipa, who was enthralled with the character dance as such, overloaded the ballet with numbers that today seem archaic and inevitably associated with operatic divertissements. Misha tossed out the so-called Gypsy number, with its showy vulgarity reminiscent of the Soviet stage. In place of its bellicose gaiety, there appeared the correct, although not very expressive, dance of Basil with the Gypsy man and woman. It was dressed up with elements of the Russian folk dance—leaps over a scarf, the Gypsy woman's number with the two partners imitating a Russian troika ride.

From the point of view of direction, the second scene of the first act is the most difficult. For Baryshnikov, it was important somehow to

Rehearsal with Elena Tchernichova / BLIOKH

justify Don Quixote's appearance in the Gypsy camp and his bout
with the windmill. In Petipa's Petersburg version, the crazed knight
threw himself on it without fear or rancor, because he had seen the
moon weeping and this evoked the desire to protect it from the giants
—for which he mistook the flapping sails of the mill. A similarly naïve
motivation in the spirit of the ballet aesthetics of the 1870s would
hardly have been suitable. Instead, Baryshnikov introduced the mimed
character of Dulcinea, the Don's "beautiful lady," who he perceives as
a prisoner of the evil windmill. An intentional stylization of Goya's
majas, she emerges as a phantom beckoning Don Quixote to justify his
quest, at least within the framework of the ballet. At the end, seen only
by her knight, she passes along the edge of the stage amid the ferment
of the wedding festivities to entice the Don to undertake his search for
his *"princesse lointaine."*

In the second scene, Dulcinea acts as fabricator of Don Quixote's
dream, in the manner of a beautiful chatelaine giving a festival of the

classical dance in his honor. In the old versions, in particular the one
the Kirov uses, the sprightly village girl Kitri flits before Don
Quixote's eyes as a new Dulcinea. Here, Petipa was playing with the
democratic mood of the Russian audience, which, after the emancipa-
tion of the serfs, was fascinated by the idea of "peasant queens." The
notion seemed farfetched to Baryshnikov. So, in Don Quixote's dream,
Kitri figures as a real character who has wandered momentarily into
the knight's dreamy fantasy of Dulcinea.

The dream itself is Petipa's tribute to the standard romantic device

After the première of *Don
Quixote*, in Washington, D.C.
/ PHOTO © BY LEONID LUBI-
ANITSKY

of Saint-Léon, who loved to introduce "unreal divertissements" into his ballets. In Baryshnikov's version, the dream acquires a certain logic for the first time: Don Quixote dreams of his ideal, Dulcinea, in the company of unearthly beauties, among whom Amour appears fleetingly. He is treated ironically, picking up the tone of the prologue, as he strikes vaudeville masks with his arrows. This distinguishes Baryshnikov's from the Kirov's canonical version, where the dream is drawn out as a rather insipid divertissement. That Baryshnikov's dream appears against the background of the windmill and not in a romantic no-

man's-land renders it even more convincing. Dulcinea is in the mill and comes down to evoke the dances that follow.

The dream scene has one other side. Baryshnikov not only constructed it as part of a vaudeville in full swing but also gave it an unmistakable concert-hall chic. And in this connection, Elena Tchernichova was a great help to him. She is a former Kirov ballerina, a teacher and choreographer, who like Baryshnikov was thoroughly sick of the Kirov's academic dream. Elena recalled fondly the work on *Don Quixote* with Baryshnikov. "Misha's a wonderful director, and he has the ability to demonstrate each character. He did Gamache and Amour and Sancho for the troupe with such relish and such humor everybody practically died laughing. What he had done in the Kirov, in dancing Basil with an obviously ironic attitude toward the vaudeville silliness, he took as the key to the direction. He demanded the same approach to their roles from the dancers. That's probably why Victor Barbee's Gamach was so successful, as were John Meehan's Espada and Alexander Minz's Quixote. They were fashioned like masks in the *commedia dell'arte*."

Acts II and III in Baryshnikov's *Don Quixote* may seem a "cascade of dance after dance that filled the stage" or "wall-to-wall motion," as critics put it. But the most remarkable thing about them is the way they are structured with the consistency of musical comedy or vaudeville, demanding that the action develop at high speed, without letting the audience take a breath. For the sake of *Don Quixote*'s compressed action, Baryshnikov eliminated many of the mass dances Petipa's version abounds in—the tedious fandango, or Mercedes's solo in the last act, for instance. To his credit, Baryshnikov as Basil hasn't allowed himself much sustained dancing. Originally Basil's part was mostly mime, and throughout the century his interpreters—from Mikhail Mordkin to Vladimir Vasiliev—helped to build up its choreographic flesh. To Basil's traditional patterns Baryshnikov modestly added an imaginative "drunken solo" in Act II, danced with wine cups in hand, laced with Baryshnikov's dazzling double *sauts de basque*.

He was mostly concerned with weaving his Basil into the joyful, frolicsome texture of the action, without making his virtuosity and impish charm stand out in the conventional Spanish crowd. Probably his greatest achievement in both acts is the way he "displays an instinctive skill in apportioning the dancing and the small groups—toreadors and their responsively flashy ladies, perky flower girls, amiable village youths—who fluently succeed each other, circling and zigzagging across the open space, are clearly differentiated, their characters pinpointed by their movement," as dance critic Tobi Tobias noted.

In contrast to his *Nutcracker*, whose action is concentrated mostly on three protagonists, *Don Quixote* is a perfect example of ensemble ballet, where each component is equally valuable, to an even greater degree than the masked figures in *commedia dell'arte*. Kitri and Basil share their priority with the others, distinguishing Baryshnikov's version from those of the Kirov or the Bolshoi, where the main figures dazzle against the rather murky background. Due to the ensemble-like swift action, Baryshnikov managed to bring new life to the ballet that in Russia demonstrated only Kitri's bravura or Basil's clowning escapades. What is more, rather than the inappropriate Chagall-like set and scenery designed by Boris Aronson for *The Nutcracker*, *Don Quixote* unfolds within colorful sets designed by Santo Loquasto. The frothy costumes contribute to the joyful atmosphere of balletic *españolada*, and a front cloth—a painted fan depicting the verve of a bullfight—unobtrusively hints at the subsequent merry *corrida* of a loving couple fighting for their happiness despite all tricks of fortune. "I wanted the whole show to have speed and light colors . . . I wanted Goya crossed with Yves Saint Laurent. I think Santo's designs are wonderful; they make the show," Baryshnikov commented enthusiastically.

Although, since its triumphant première in Washington, D.C., on March 23, 1978, *Don Quixote* has enjoyed universal recognition, Baryshnikov continued to repeat: "I am not a choreographer . . . I keep saying it and I mean it." Asked if the experience of producing *The Nutcracker* and *Don Quixote* made him more likely to stage and choreograph more ballets, Baryshnikov stubbornly repeated an emphatic "No!" Nevertheless, as artistic director of the American Ballet Theatre, he has already started to work on a new version of *Swan Lake*. Whether it will be another experiment in balletic stage direction or a daring attempt to choreograph it from scratch, Baryshnikov so far doesn't know himself. But it will hardly be regarded as another "choreographic debut."

8 WITH BALANCHINE AND ROBBINS

IN THE FALL of 1978 Baryshnikov, golden boy of the American Ballet Theatre, created an upheaval in ballet circles by moving to the other major ballet company in New York. As Clive Barnes remarked: "It is no great deal. Just imagine President Carter declaring he was a Republican."

Possibly the thought of working with choreographer George Balanchine and the New York City Ballet occurred to Misha in the winter of 1972, when he saw the troupe on tour in Leningrad. He had missed Balanchine's sensational tour in 1962, since he was a young student in Riga at the time. Then, the combination of first-class dancers like Allegra Kent, Arthur Mitchell, Edward Villella, Diana Adams, Violette Verdy and the contemporary atmosphere that Balanchine's neoclassical compositions exuded was truly stunning.

In 1972, there were no longer such striking personalities in the troupe as before. Suzanne Farrell was dancing with Maurice Béjart in Brussels. Edward Villella was having trouble with his back and his appearance in "Rubies" was more disenchanting than exciting. Allegra Kent, who had astonished the ballet world of Leningrad with her *Sonnambula*, was absent. I can vividly recall the opening of the tour in the Palace of Industrial Cooperation (there were other performances at the Kirov). Misha was in the audience. The evening began with the old *Serenade*, far too reminiscent of Fokine for Russian eyes, and Jerry Robbins's *Scherzo Fantastique*, which was not too "scherzoso" and far from fantastic. During the entr'acte, we exchanged opinions. "So far, nothing special somehow. Rather démodé and in general not headed in the right direction . . ." Misha observed, disenchanted. This impression vanished when he saw the truly brilliant *Violin Concerto*, choreographed by Balanchine to Stravinsky. Everyone was astonished by Peter Martins's artistry, his marvelous technique, and the manliness of his dancing, which was reminiscent of the young Erik Bruhn.

Through Valery Panov, I met many of the dancers—Eddie Villella, Gelsey Kirkland, Rickey (Robert) and Cathy Weiss. I bent everyone's ear about Baryshnikov—many of the Americans had heard about his triumph in London but hadn't seen him. *The Creation of the World* was not playing then, and Misha was dancing only minor things—the hackneyed pas de deux from *Don Quixote*, *The Flames of Paris*, and *Vestris*—in a combined program for the young stars of the Kirov Ballet.

Gelsey and Rickey had seen Baryshnikov, and agreed with me that he was an absolute phenomenon. At a party at Panov's, I was repeatedly questioned: "Is he really going to stay here? How great he would be, dancing with us." Panov, having decided to leave, and incredulous that others would remain, said blithely: "Oh, he'll run off. Give him a chance to gain momentum and he'll be with everybody—Balanchine included." At the time, I was far from thinking of Panov as a prophet.

The contact with the Balanchine troupe, albeit quite superficial, continued into the autumn of 1973, when my friends the Weisses stopped by from Stockholm to see me. They wanted to take another look at Baryshnikov, if not in performance, at least in the class he was taking then with Irina Kolpakova's husband, Vladilen Semenov. In class, Baryshnikov was in great form, as was Yuri Soloviev—though the latter's self-esteem was wounded by the appearance of foreign guests to see Baryshnikov.

"He's gotten even better," Cathy remarked. "And what about his plans? Have they changed?" Rickey asked. "Talk to him about it yourselves, friends," I suggested.

We got together at Elena Tchernichova's; no doubt it never entered her head at that time that five years later Misha would be staging *Don Quixote* in America with her assistance. Nor could Rickey imagine then that in 1975 he would make his debut at the American Ballet Theatre as a choreographer by mounting *Awakening* for Baryshnikov and Gelsey Kirkland. Misha, who seemed to be flattered by the attention of Balanchine's dancers, spouted jokes, alternating them with questions about ballet life in New York and Makarova's career in particular. He listened to Rickey's report on the ballerina's tremendous success. "By the way, she gets something like three thousand dollars for a performance," he said. Misha burst out laughing. "Well, that kind of paradise is definitely not for me . . ."

Despite the front-page stories and the surprise evinced by some at Baryshnikov's switch to the New York City Ballet, collaboration with Balanchine had been anticipated by Misha's admirers and Balanchine's champions since Misha's first performance in America. Both groups strongly believed that under Balanchine's guidance a dancer of such caliber would reveal new facets of his talent, and that it would be an affront to ballet history if these two giants never collaborated. It would be as if Pavlova and Fokine had never met. For this reason, "the marriage of the old and new Maryinsky" took place in an atmosphere full of excitement, if mixed with skepticism among those who knew of Balanchine's policy with ballet stars. The experience of established stars who found themselves in Balanchine's galaxy—Erik Bruhn, for instance—was often far from satisfactory.

Misha's statements in the press were enthusiastic, nevertheless. "I would love to be an instrument in his wonderful hands . . . The repertory of the New York City Ballet is enormous. I have so many opportunities to try myself out . . . Slowly I realized that I would never forgive myself if I did not try. I am thirty, with a few years left."

To the public, puzzled by his taxing choice, he replied: "If there is a part of the public that is disappointed that they will not see me in *Don Quixote* or *Giselle*, I'll say, 'Go see *The Turning Point.*' It's like a marriage . . . I feel as if I am in a church, and in church you do not think of divorce."

To some people, bemused at his financial sacrifice—from $3,000 to $5,000 for a single performance at ABT to $750 a week—and his acceptance of the first-among-equals situation, Misha said: "I did not come to the States to make money. It's a good thing, but not the main one . . . As for my superstar position, it really doesn't mean very much to me. Celebrity is like having extra sugar in your coffee."

Mr. Balanchine, whose only indisputable star is his own choreography, reported in his reserved and matter-of-fact way: "He is gifted . . . He has good feet . . ."

Balanchine's choreography can be rightly considered the last turn of that extended Russian spiral which encompassed Baryshnikov's first six years in the West. Balanchine offered him the ultimate challenge, tempting him for reasons far beyond any desire to become the first among the Russian ballet superstars accepted in the Balanchine ballet community. (This honor was not bestowed upon Nureyev or Makarova.) The acceptance certainly flattered Baryshnikov's ego, but it was not a major impetus to his move. Few penetrated the real sense of Baryshnikov's enthusiastic announcement in the press: "I am entering the ideal future of the Maryinsky ballet, two hundred years ahead. Some people here are skeptical about it, but my Russian friends will understand at once and rejoice. In Russia, Balanchine is an incredible symbol of uncompromised creative genius."

Like many of his compatriots, Misha regarded Balanchine's achievement as the modern crystallization of Russian balletic classicism that was destined to flourish only beyond native boundaries. His work was the unfulfilled future of Russian ballet, the artistic experience of which bypassed Soviet Russia. In America Misha could not resist the temptation of Balanchine. Psychologically his affiliation with the New York City Ballet would be the supreme justification for his defection, giving a special sense to it. By joining Balanchine's company, he in a way was returning to the old Maryinsky in its brand-new hypostasis.

There was another side to working with Balanchine that was attractive. Baryshnikov's development in the West was so spectacular that, at thirty, the leading classical dancer in the world seemed to have hit his peak. In his work, the balance between artistry and classical technique was ideal, so much so that further development as an artist seemed out of the question. His youth notwithstanding, Baryshnikov was experiencing the weariness of a master. His former roles carried with them the danger of self-repetition, which was all the more undesirable as the demands he made upon himself grew, as did his audiences' expectation of constant miracles. What he did outside ABT, working sporadically with Eliot Feld or Paul Taylor for instance, guaranteed him only partial self-realization. Balanchine offered him a mass of difficulties in the areas of both technique and style. Misha wanted these hardships, as a king might sometimes want to be a day laborer.

George Balanchine's personality was highly attractive as well: his meticulous Petersburg speech, dry humor, elegant clarity of judgment, and rich cultural background reminded Baryshnikov of his Kirov teacher and father-figure, Pushkin. Balanchine was perceived by Misha as part of Europeanized Russian culture, dedicated to twentieth-century figures of culture like Stravinsky and Nabokov. "He's marvelous," Misha told me. "In his judgments there's something wise and childlike at the same time. 'You dress girls up in nice costumes, teach them to dance, and, you know, it works out very nicely sometimes.' He lives in the most remarkable way, very ascetically—no excess furniture, nothing superfluous, not even a record player. And, at the same time, he's such a Russian Grand Seigneur, aesthete, and gourmet. It's as if all the culture he has stored up inside him is enough and there is nothing he needs from outside."

The troupe's monastic discipline, reminiscent of the Kirov in Sergeyev's day, and Balanchine's image of an absolute monarch in the best traditions of Petipa and Diaghilev, also cast an enticing and nostalgic patina on the harsh realities. The difficulties that lay ahead were immense—the new technique, the new style, a repertoire designed primarily for female dancers, the lack of suitable partners.

Like many of his friends, Misha thought the switch from Petipa's technique to Balanchine's idiom would be a smooth one. His successful previous experience with *Apollo*, *The Prodigal Son*, and with *Theme and Variations* at ABT encouraged him. *Apollo* and *The Prodigal Son* seemed to offer him "purely stylistic problems," as he put it. As for *Theme and Variations*, it was, according to him, just "an amplitude of steps from the precise combinations of classical routine. In the good sense, it's banal. You have double *rond de jambe*, *sissonnes battues*. It's just physically exhausting." During the first performances of *Theme* in October 1974 in Washington, D.C., he thought his "legs would drop off." As he recorded in *Baryshnikov at Work*:

> There is a continuous stream of demi-plié and plié, down, up, down, up, tension, release, tension, release. And that, coupled with working from a very accentuated turn-out at all times, means that the strain on the legs is incredible. The choreography for the male variations requires a certain unrelenting level of energy; there is very little rest, a constant build to the climax. One diagonal of very difficult beats leads immediately into a continuously repeated beat-*sissonne* combination and then into seven double tours alternating with pirouettes, ending with a multiple pirouette.

In comparison with Petipa's technique in male dancing, said Misha in *Ballet News*, "all the beats are without preparation. Usually, in Romantic ballets, the beats are not small; Balanchine took a lot of beats from Bournonville. They are not typical of the Russian School where you have bigger beats with greater preparation."

That Balanchine considered posing in preparation a cardinal sin to be avoided at all costs didn't bother Misha. His own highly concentrated dancing—a double pirouette or an air turn seemed to be linking steps without preparation—promised the swift mastering of the new style. His fabulous coordination might provide the ability to cope with the density of movements and the syncopated rhythm, to sustain balance from one position to another and to turn the other way just when the momentum is going in the opposite direction. But probably the most tempting task, from Misha's point of view, was to master the so-called impersonal style of performing, which had nothing in common with his Russian schooling. When I worked with Natalia Makarova on *A Dance Autobiography*, it cost us tremendous effort to define this major feature of Balanchine's choreography and its staccato-like style: "[It] does not come to Russian dancers easily, because our approach to performing movements is quite different. We are taught to feel our muscles by executing steps that seem to be passing through our whole body, and after being felt they demand to be emotionally expressed by the body through pure classical means. Least of all we are apt to dance mechanically, whereas Balanchine's style is based on a mechanical technique whose virtuoso combinations are given to the body as its main task to undertake and perform."

That is why, in tackling Balanchine's style, Misha had to struggle against the Russian way of performing, which practically ran in his blood. To a certain degree it was supposed to be the last hard blow by Baryshnikov against himself—his image of a Russian virtuoso, his theatrical instincts and devices.

To understand why the Balanchine-Baryshnikov collaboration turned out to be only partially fruitful, it's worthwhile to scrutinize Balanchine's aesthetics and some principles of his choreographic style.

As an artist Balanchine was a legitimate offspring of the Russian imperial style fostered by Marius Petipa, and his aesthetics took shape under the aegis of Serge Diaghilev's balletic innovations. Petipa, Diaghilev, and Balanchine form a triad. They encompass the classical ballet as a whole, but, to a certain extent, each link in this triad both derives from and renounces the others.

To say that Balanchine's neoclassic ballet sprang from Petipa's aesthetics and Diaghilev's Seasons is tantamount to repeating William Faulkner's dictum that all American literature emerged from Mark Twain's *Huckleberry Finn*. It is to say everything while saying nothing. And it is more so when applied to the art of ballet, an art form whose artificial language does not lend itself to natural development as readily as literature does. The dictum that "art evolves not out of continuity, but in spite of it" can be applied to ballet only in reference to the revamping of fundamentals. And these, the very language of classical ballet, had just been postulated by its creator, Marius Petipa, at the end of the nineteenth century. The mark of Diaghilev's genius was in his understanding that it would be premature to subject this still newly born language to drastic reforms.

Within a span of fifty creative years in Russia (1847–1900), Marius Petipa created the academic balletic vocabulary. He developed a highly polyphonic structure in choreography equivalent to that of music (in his ballet to Tchaikovsky's *The Sleeping Beauty*), but as visual art, his ballets were lacking. As spectacle, ballet was still lagging somewhere in the nineteenth century on the level of "visual delight" for Victorian habitués assessing the dancers' legs. To turn ballet into anything comparable to the theater at the beginning of the twentieth century was clearly beyond Petipa's means. That would call for a synthesis of music, painting, and dance, rather than dance per se. The dance, of course, was there; but Russian painting of the time was predominantly realistic and artists' experience with theater sets was nil. Ballet music, in its turn, with the exception of that by Tchaikovsky and Glazunov, was warbling on the level of Offenbach.

With the unique intuition of a great innovator, Diaghilev understood that rivalry among the arts ultimately results in progress. Throughout the centuries the arts have vied to appropriate each other's characteristics, devices, and techniques. Unremittingly, they have been involved in the incestuous absorption of each other's features, in order, finally, to realize the singularity of their own artistic sphere. (Thus cinema, after having passed through a period of rivalry with dramatic theater, music-hall shows, and even circus acts, became aware of its own field, as distinct from the other arts.)

In order to boost the popularity of ballet within the family of the arts, Diaghilev had to create a ballet spectacle, a feast for the eyes, rivaling in its picturesqueness any other form of depiction, including painting. That is why his prewar Saisons Russes (1909–12) were developed with the collaboration of Mikhail Fokine. Fokine's romantic vignettes (*Les Sylphides, Le Spectre de la Rose, Le Pavillon d'Armide*) were decorative, aesthetic stylizations, a nostalgic sigh for the evanescent world of Marie Taglioni and Carlotta Grisi. Or they were simply animated fairy-tale-like images with whimsical subjects (*Petrouchka* and *Cléopâtre*). Alexandre Benois and Léon Bakst, Diaghilev's companions since the publication of his magazine *Mir Iskusstva* (*The World of Art*) in 1899, created for him sets and costumes that played a functional, not subsidiary, role on stage. They shared the success with Nijinsky and Karsavina's dancing and Fokine's choreography. These ballet performances and theatrical shows took Paris by storm. The artistry was of such a high level that neither Diaghilev in his postwar

Seasons, nor his followers in England and France, could later match it.
By the time the fourth Season started (1912), Diaghilev realized
that the idea of ballet as a parallel of painting had essentially been used
up. For this reason he put Fokine in the shadow and pushed Nijinsky
the choreographer into the footlights, with his *Après-midi d'un Faune*
and *Le Sacre du Printemps*. Dance took a turn from the illustrative to
the almost abstract, though, for the time being, it retained the umbili-
cal cord of a plot.

For more than fifteen years, Diaghilev led dance in the direction of
non-pictorial expressiveness, until it became completely autonomous.
This new ballet trend based on pure dance was created slowly and
painfully. Dozens of ephemera, such as *The Blue Train, Barabau*,
and *La Pastorale*, had to be tried before the birth of *Apollo* (1928)
and *The Prodigal Son* (1929), choreographed by George Balanchine.
These works were a summing up of Diaghilev's activities, and they
opened the door to the future of ballet.

The unique equilibrium created by Prokofiev's music, Rouault's
visual works, and Balanchine's choreography excluded any rivalry
among the components of *The Prodigal Son*. All three were equally
important. *Apollo* marked the beginning of the era of neoclassic dance
—movement prevailed over the visual accouterments of a performance, and was subordinate only to the music.

The concept of dance as a visual parallel to music was, for a time,
vital. It became the basis of Frederick Ashton's ballets in the 1930s and
stimulated the development of the ballet in England, which had formerly been feeding only on crumbs from the banquet of imperial
Russian ballet. Neoclassicism, however, did not become the main trend
in English ballet. It did become the main characteristic of the choreography of Diaghilev's spiritual son, George Balanchine. He was the only
one in Diaghilev's Saisons Russes who became truly innovative according to its principles.

Many members of the New York City Ballet greeted Misha with a
flattering "Welcome home," hinting that he was a prodigal son returning to his native, though quite reshaped, Maryinsky. Their words
echoed the remark of George Balanchine himself, who in 1962 at
Sheremetyevo Airport in Moscow, in response to the Soviet greetings
—"Welcome to Moscow, home of the classical ballet"—replied: "I beg

your pardon. Russia is the home of Romantic ballet. The home of classic ballet is now in America." No matter how his statement might tickle the American ear, it is at variance with historical facts, Romantic ballet emerged in France in 1830, and, of course, the first Giselle was interpreted not by Elena Andreyanova, the famous Russian Giselle of the forties and fifties, but by Carlotta Grisi, for whom the Frenchman Jules Perrot choreographed the patterns. As for the illustrious *La Sylphide*, it was created in Paris by Philippe Taglioni for his daughter Marie, but in Russia this ballet appeared through the efforts of the French choreographer Antoine Titus. Marius Petipa emerged from the Romantic aesthetics of his day to work out the academic grammar of classical dance. This grammar was fostered in St. Petersburg–Leningrad, blossoming there in a span of a hundred years, until the 1960s, after which it went into abrupt decline. Balanchine's neoclassical vocabulary used Petipa's legacy as a springboard. Its kinship is in a certain academism, if this concept connotes a definite number of elaborate balletic steps, devices, and attitudes. Its home is New York.

Balanchine employed the Petipa grammar in his own way. Its fundamentals, be it arabesque, *pas de chat*, or cabriole, don't contain any emotional message. They are basically formal and only within the workings of a storytelling ballet did they serve a plot, conveying a certain meaning. The basis of classical ballet is not emotional and its steps are pure convention. Balanchine capitalized on this particular quality of classical dancing. By doing away with its storytelling function, which became the major feature of Soviet ballet, Balanchine emphasized classical fundamentals and achieved their metamorphosis, as Serge Diaghilev had dreamed of doing.

The lack of classical tradition in America in a way stimulated this creative process. To inculcate the imperial style, Balanchine had to make classical dancing "recognizable" for the public at large, to adapt it for Americans, brought up on tap, jazz, and Broadway-like shows. In other words, on the aesthetics of "pure motion," when the dancing body, its muscular knack, its lines and sex appeal, provides aesthetic bliss. He sacrificed the legato of Russian schooling and replaced it with fast rhythms and the syncopation of jazz.

Boris Pasternak loved to quote the words of Stefan George about Dante: "He turned the past [i.e., the poetic tradition] into ashes, then blew, and created *Inferno* out of them." In terms of ballet, Balanchine produced the same miracle. By throwing away the legato, he put

Petipa's grammar on a different rhythm, cut the links that created the flowing transition of one movement into another. There were no longer obviously main steps and their preparations: they blended into one dense stream of movement, performed to a swift tempo in a relatively short period of time. Emphasis was put on pointwork, while the position of the arms (the most time-consuming area in the classical education) was neglected. He enriched Petipa's vocabulary with elements of early Romantic technique (mostly Bournonville), tap dancing, jazz, and American show business. Essentially he followed the Petipa steps, borrowing, as Petipa had, from other traditions. *Pas emboîté*, embellishing the compositions in *La Bayadère* and *The Sleeping Beauty*, was borrowed by Petipa from the Offenbach cancan. In the 1860s, during his short visit to Paris, Petipa tried to astonish the Paris Opera with the charming skill of his young wife Maria Surovshchikova in his early ballets. He failed to startle the Parisians, but the cancan steps did not escape the notice of less blasé St. Petersburg balletomanes.

Due to the speed, rhythm, and lack of linking movements, the old classical grammar acquired a new dimension of highly concentrated dancing, which was an astonishing phenomenon per se. To judge Balanchine's technique using Petipa's criteria (as they do in England) is, after all, like measuring the technique of Vladimir Nabokov using Tolstoy's standards. The successor can in neither case be considered "deteriorated."

Nevertheless, during the tour of the New York City Ballet in London in 1979, both their style and their technique became targets for critical attack. As G. B. L. Wilson put it in *Dance News*:

In Mr. Balanchine's work so often the arms and hands seem overstretched and straining for something—which at first sight offends us . . . Similarly our hips must always be level—to be otherwise is an affront to sensibility. And when we see one of Mr. Balanchine's girls raise her leg vertically and raise her hip to get it there, a shiver of horror runs through the audience (so many of whom are students, teachers and dancers). But it is in the use of the hands and arms that our dissent is greatest. Our preparation for a turn demands a curved arm before us with the hand following the curve, fingers held together. Our American friends horrify us with fingers sticking out, a flick of the wrist on the turn (one of our critics wrote of *Symphony in C*, "The corps de ballet was a ballet master's nightmare with hands and arms all over the place") and a general irregularity above the shoulders which suggests that the arms and hands have not been choreographed at all—only the feet and legs! We are interested, too, in the way the dancers turn, with all the weight on a straight supporting leg, whereas we prepare by slightly flexing the knees and with the weight equally on both legs to begin with . . .

The list of these divergences can easily be supplemented, but such critical arrows bypass the target. Balanchine's technique perfectly serves his style, contributing to the creation of "disinterested beauty" —movements for the sake of their beauty, not just for precision. Possibly the most audacious achievement of Balanchine is the way he employs the corps de ballet. In Petipa's system, its compositions are mostly frontal. They reveal the penchant of the old maestro for Cartesian precision, harmony of proportion, peacefulness. Petipa's corps is a noble, humanistic accompaniment, indirectly mimicking classical sculpture, in motion or at rest. Balanchine's corps is usually divided into groups, each of which pursues its own pattern: they operate in disunity, based on syncopation. Out of their unity, chaotic at first glance, somehow emerges a special harmony of disharmony, endemic to the music of Alban Berg, Igor Stravinsky, and Sergei Prokofiev. The stage, filled with the moving members of the corps, can be likened to abstract painting in motion, which demands a special perception to appreciate it. Balanchine intellectualized the balletic stage space, thereby transforming it into a phenomenon of visual perception endemic to the twentieth century.

In his ballets of the 1940s—*Concerto Barocco* (1941), *The Four Temperaments* (1946), *Symphony in C* (1947), and *Theme and Variations* (1947)—dance per se not only became a visual delight because of the particular beauty of its choreographic compositions but seemed to absorb the intellectual energy of music, strictly corresponding to its abstract content. It provided an equivalent choreographic structure and became a kind of hieroglyph. Ballet as art ceased to compete with its contingent brothers, such as dramatic theater or painting, and, at its best, even beat the music, as in Balanchine's *Symphony in C* (Bizet) or *Pas de Deux* (Tchaikovsky). By inducing a certain intellectualization rather than merely the enjoyment of visual effects, Balanchine seemed to help ballet realize the final step in its evolution—the self-assurance necessary to define its own sphere—pure dancing without any message.

The dancers in his ballets can be rightly likened to the colorful strokes of an abstract painting—their intensity surely depends more on the dancers' physical qualities than on their projection. Edwin Denby, in his time the most perceptive ballet critic in America, incisively noted that Balanchine "had to find a way for Americans to look grand and noble, yet not be embarrassed by it. The Russian way is for each dancer to feel what he is expressing. The Americans weren't ready to do that. By concentrating on form and the whole ensemble Balanchine was able to bypass the uncertainties of the individual dancer."

Baryshnikov was hardly bothered by stagefright, and Balanchine's emphasis on the whole ensemble threatened to jeopardize his personality. The challenge for him consisted in placing himself within the confines of Balanchine's style and in bringing his leanings toward detachment to the fore. But there was another stumbling block—the priority of female dancing in Balanchine's ballets. In this Balanchine is a direct successor of Petipa, whose choreography is primarily a triumph of female dancing, inherited from the age of Romanticism. But as a follower, Balanchine went much further.

W. H. Auden once wrote that the idea of time is basically alien to classical ballets. The action takes place in Eden, a world of pure delight, devoid of human passions, destructiveness, and grief. The plot intricacies might imply suffering, but they are puppet-like. In classical ballet, as in fairy tales, there is neither the past nor the future, even if the time limits are defined, as in *The Sleeping Beauty*. Classical ballet is a continuum of bliss, visually incarnating the idea of Paradise—a realm of sinlessness, beyond good or evil.

Balanchine's plotless ballets conjure up this realm. Their focus on the ballerina's supremacy, deriving essentially from the Romantic concept of woman, underscored the idea of Paradise. Most of his ballets are plunged in a kind of before-the-fall atmosphere as the partners enjoy their dreamy mutual detachment. No wonder his choreography is basically devoid of blatant sexual implications—Romanticism is asexuality par excellence. As Croce noted: "For Balanchine it is the man who sees and follows and it is the woman who acts and guides."

With his spirited temperament, Baryshnikov was hardly apt at playing the role of a passive observer. The choreographic paucity of male parts in Balanchine's repertory confined, rather than helped to release, his forte. Because of his ballet upbringing and psychological structure, he was more inclined to enjoy the upper hand in partnering. One of his chief virtues is his ability to sustain dramatic tension in a performance from beginning to end, and the majority of Balanchine's ballets supplied him with piecemeal participation at best.

Except for his role in Roland Petit's *The Queen of Spades*, Misha spent the fall of 1978 working intensively on Balanchine's repertoire, rehearsing over fifteen ballets at once. Dedicating himself to this task, he even put off his Nijinsky film project for the time being (and has yet to turn back to it). He had had some problems picking the right director for the movie—Franco Zeffirelli spoke highly of the screenplay by Misha and Carl Black, but was unable to tackle it immediately; other candidates had turned out to be unavailable. But in November of 1978 this didn't upset Baryshnikov. He was utterly immersed in his new roles, relishing every moment of his endless rehearsals. On November 14, 1978, he opened the New York City Ballet season with "Rubies."

This is the most dynamic section of the Balanchine triptych *Jewels* and, in my opinion, the most successful. The choreography is built on the ragged, staccato, syncopated music of Stravinsky, and seems to reproduce the image of rubies—the constantly changing, bewitching glimmer. Rubies are vulgar stones compared to emeralds and diamonds, whose more noble images come through in the classically polished, almost traditional, choreographic sketches devoted to them in *Jewels*. Their combinations intentionally lack innovative brilliance, and refer to Petipa's lexicon in *Raymonda* and *The Sleeping Beauty*.

Baryshnikov, with his mercurial, driving technique capable of coping with any tempo, was a real find as a performer of "Rubies." But the choreography, which provides for elements of jazz dancing (hops, dashes, sharp turns of the body on bent legs) as well as classical movements, is a dangerous trap. The temptation is to play up this peculiarly charming eclecticism, with its dash of chic vulgarity verging on a parody of jazz. But, as always with Balanchine, the idea permeating the choreography acquires additional dimensions only if it is danced without an emotional attitude toward it. It is only a matter of, let's say, playing with it ironically, for the work to take on an exaggerated pointedness that is quite out of place. The "idea of rubies" is realized in an ensemble of dancers who create a certain shifting, colored unity that acquires an intellectual dimension that can be interpreted in any way one pleases.

In his first performance, on November 14, 1978, Baryshnikov danced "Rubies" with a Russian approach to the choreography: he introduced an emotional coloration into his execution. In several spots, he tried to be comic, thrashing about amusingly in place, as if he had lost his partner, Patricia McBride. Or he started to work with excessive intensity, his pelvis giving the dance sexual overtones. This naturally evoked laughter, and many in the New York audience associated Ba-

"Rubies," with Patricia McBride / MARTHA SWOPE

ryshnikov's performance with his earlier New York appearance in Twyla Tharp's humorous *Push Comes to Shove*. But in *Push*, fun is deliberately poked at the affected nature of the routine poses and positions of classical ballet. In "Rubies," this sort of comic treatment cheapened the intellectual game of the ballet, rendering its abstract qualities inappropriately concrete. In short, a stylistic absurdity resulted.

The ballets that derive more from Balanchine's Russian heritage, such as *Coppélia*, *The Prodigal Son*, and *Apollo*, provided a smoother transition for Baryshnikov.

He made his debut in Balanchine's version of *Coppélia*—the most imaginative and well-structured readaptation of Saint-Léon–Petipa's antediluvian relic—in Saratoga in July 1978. The part of Franz, who dances mainly in a first-act solo and a coda in the Franz-Swanilda pas de deux in Act III (both are Balanchine's additions to the choreography), didn't contain anything blatantly new to Baryshnikov. He was the same flamboyant flirt that he had portrayed earlier in an insipid American Ballet Theatre production of *Coppélia*. Perhaps this time his Franz became a more integral part of the pastoral comedy—one of its main adornments rather than its major virtuoso.

The Prodigal Son, which he had learned in Geneva with Balanchine's former ballerina Patricia Neary in 1977, challenged him with a broader range of possibilities. It is one of Balanchine's undisputed masterpieces, although, created fifty years ago in Diaghilev's era, the ballet doesn't benefit from the nostalgic haze of time. Much of the choreography no longer looks as audacious as it did to the audience of 1929. Its vocabulary calls to mind the innovations of Kasyan Goleizovsky, who, in the turbulent twenties in Russia, infused the petrified classical lexicon with borrowings from gymnasts, acrobats, and circus performers, and was greatly admired by the young Balanchine as a creator of "Youth Ballet" in Petrograd.

The Rouault sets and costumes have now lost a bit of their daring charm; the revelers' bustle with the pitchers is as pedestrian and obtrusive as are the exuberance of phallic symbols in the ballet. But still impressive are the gamut of colors, highly appropriate to a balletic transcription of the parable from St. Luke; the monstrous, hairless revelers whose entangled bodies and arachnidian plasticity torment the virginal youth; the retreat of the revelers as if sailing away, led by the Siren, who is arched backward in the pose of a figurehead; and the final

The Prodigal Son / MARTHA SWOPE

biblical enfolding of the panic-stricken boy by his austere but forgiving father.

The choreography came to Baryshnikov easily, but the part was complicated by the general expectation that he compete with the incomparable Edward Villella's Prodigal Son. Truly exemplary in terms of style and personal projection, Villella portrayed more a potential warrior than a frivolous rake annoyed by domestic routine. A restrained manner was punctuated by solemn outbursts of suppressed tempestuosity. Baryshnikov was entirely different—more childish and vulnerable, more a lost boy of Mantegna than a tortured youth of Rembrandt. His characterization was less stylized and more spontaneous. He seemed to sweep through the part with genuine involvement. Some personal qualities, fury and vulnerability, lurked behind his rebellious jumps and the stunning turns in the first solo. He imbued the role with his impulsive humor, something that never marked Villella's interpretation. It came through especially in the duet between the Siren and the Prodigal Son that Agnes de Mille once deemed "one of the most important seductions to be found on any modern stage." Baryshnikov seemed to laugh off his effort to cope with the enormous seductress, wrapping herself around his waist like a snake, towering over him like a bird of prey during the promenades.

Some critics found fault with Baryshnikov's Prodigal Son because of his departure from Balanchine's impersonal style. But Diaghilev, an instigator of the ballet, amazed its first cast by demanding that they give free hand to emotional outpouring, so in this respect Baryshnikov's interpretation was stylistically impeccable.

If something marred his portrayal, it was his new costume, a kind of loose overall, suggested by Balanchine. This untimely innovation merely hindered Baryshnikov's movements and disfigured his lines. It was all the more regrettable that he appeared in the television special *Dance in America* in this grotesque attire.

Another badly timed innovation was Balanchine's sudden decision to reconstruct *Apollo*, turning it into a plotless ballet. The original 1928 *Apollo* fully corresponded to Baryshnikov's dancing potential and his theatrical instincts. His interpretation of the role, shown at the Chicago Ballet Festival in 1978 and previously in Paris, was far superior to his première at the New York City Ballet in May 1979. Although the Chicago version was slightly truncated, Misha was still permitted to dance Apollo's first solo, a dance of self-discovery in which he used

The Prodigal Son, with Karin
Aroldingen / MARTHA SWOPE

Apollo, Chicago Ballet Festival, 1978, with Allegra Kent / BLIOKH

the lute as a toy, and the consistency of the plot, unfolding in total accordance with the myth, was preserved.

According to Homer, Apollo was an impulsive and tempestuous youth. Only after spending a year at hard labor in the sheepfolds of King Admetus did he begin to preach moderation, choosing for his motto: "Nothing in excess!" Afterward he brought the Muses down from their home on Mount Helicon to Delphi, tamed their frenzy, was educated by them, and then led them in formal and decorous dances.

In the Chicago Ballet Festival version, the mythical pattern came through. Baryshnikov's interpretation of his turbulent god was a visual metaphor of balletic classicism, opposed to its modernistic revisions. Despite some critics' complaints about Baryshnikov's "angry-young-man style," his effort to imbue Apollo's interpretation with genuinely Russian theatricality seems to me more than justifiable.

The illustrious quality of *Apollo* and its various links with storytelling ballet perhaps annoyed its creator. Cutting *Apollo* down to almost comic-strip dimensions, Balanchine settled accounts, obliquely, with his Russian past. The truncated version of *Apollo* omits the Prologue and the stairway that had come to stand for Mount Olympus. We no longer see Leto on a high platform heaving in childbirth; Apollo, unwrapped from his swaddling clothes by two handmaidens, does not open his mouth to mime the howl of an infant or take his first fearful steps. He does not receive the mysterious gift of a lute from the handmaidens. Stravinsky's score, *Apollon Musagète*, was also cut, to its detriment. These regrettable vivisections would be quite excusable if they had given birth to a brand-new Apollo. Alas, this did not happen. By liberating Apollo from his midwives and the old balletic diapers, Balanchine also liberated his ballet from Apollo himself. Now the ballet is both plotless and anonymous.

On May 1, 1979, the curtain rose on an Apollo who had already been transformed into a god of measure and moderation. Clad in white tights instead of the usual black ones, Apollo-Baryshnikov was standing in the noble pose, strumming his lute with great rotating gestures. His encounter with the Muses followed. Oddly enough, there emerged an undeniable interrelation between the excised form of the ballet and the impeccability of classical presentation Baryshnikov was radiating.

If in the former version Baryshnikov emphasized the development of Apollo as a character, now he began to convey one of the main ideas of the ballet—self-discovery through dancing. Apollo-Baryshnikov seemed to be testing his already established aesthetic creed through dances with the Muses. Since the finale in the original version had become its beginning, the taming of and by the Muses does not make any sense. As if knowing this, Baryshnikov, supporting each Muse with subdued courtesy, did not even look at them. He seemed to be testing the new ability of his muscles. (Incidentally, the Muses do not look like ribald inspirations in the present version of *Apollo*; they resemble instead the handmaidens who were deleted, in a way substituting for the absence of the hapless servants.) Apollo-Baryshnikov could dance with anyone to test his body.

Deborah Jowitt in her review in *The Village Voice* observed: "In his solo, when he brushes one leg across himself to the side and swings both arms in the opposite direction, he emphasizes neither the jazzy asymmetry nor the archaic two-dimensionality of the step, but shows with fierce zest how one part of the body is pulling against another." Through use of emotional details Baryshnikov exploded the brand-new abstractness of the ballet, trying to give it a certain sense.

The Nutcracker, Harlequinade, and *The Steadfast Tin Soldier* were ballets related in one way or another to Baryshnikov's Russian days. Misha danced the latter two quite frequently; fragments from *Harlequinade* and the complete *Soldier* were presented on television, giving a mass audience the chance to become acquainted with Baryshnikov in Balanchine's repertoire.

All three of these compositions could be nicely put together under the general heading *Jeux d'Enfants,* after the Bizet gallop that is included in *The Soldier.* These are more Balanchine's children's pieces than works for adult lovers of his intellectual ballets. Using Baryshnikov in these compositions was a kind of tribute to the Maryinsky alma mater. Balanchine's nostalgic remakes (*The Nutcracker* and *Harlequinade*) put both the choreographer and the performer into the atmosphere of the balletic delight that so thrilled the aristocratic balletomanes who once crowded the parterre of the imperial theater. But what was for Balanchine an elegaic glance back to his youth was for Baryshnikov a return to the past he was trying to forget. It was as if a university student had been given an ABC primer by a whimsical tutor.

Harlequinade was composed in 1900 by the eighty-year-old Petipa

Harlequinade / JOYCE JAFFE

and was a trifle intended for the small Hermitage Theater rather than for the regular stage. Although the masters of the Petersburg School danced in it (Nikolai Legat, Mikhail Fokine, Anna Pavlova, and Mathilde Kschessinska), it was forgotten in Russia soon after the première. Its contemporary remake is the whim of a refined choreographer who was attracted to Drigo's rather hopeless music. In the context of Balanchine's sophisticated repertoire, it looks strange, at the very least. The choreography is paltry for Balanchine, a reworking of the *commedia dell'arte* with a French sauce that is not sufficiently piquant. In *Harlequinade*, Baryshnikov had to hark back to his position at the Kirov—the choreography's inadequacies were to be compensated for by his brilliance as a dancer (especially with his legendary grand pirouette) and by that piercing lyrical note that he brought to the mask of Harlequin *mal aimé*. But after his *Coppélia*, *La Fille Mal Gardée*, and *Push Comes to Shove* at ABT, his performance in *Harlequinade* didn't even look like self-repetition; it seemed more like a Stradivarius playing a gallop at an amateur concert for children. The critics were enthusiastic, while those who truly knew Baryshnikov's work expressed legitimate doubts. The role was clearly not up to his potential and hardly enriched either him or the audience.

The same impression was left by *The Nutcracker*, which, fortunately, he danced only a few times. In the final pas de deux, the male role is one of pure partnering, and throughout there was little opportunity for Baryshnikov to dance. It was almost as if casting of this kind were meant to compromise his image, both as a virtuoso and as the intellectual dancer that he had come to be in the West.

The Steadfast Tin Soldier reaffirmed this impression, although one critic thought that "Baryshnikov's terse staccato style transformed *The Steadfast Tin Soldier* from a minor work into a major gem." The ballet is based on one of the most touching of Andersen's fairy tales, telling of the love of a tin soldier for a paper-doll ballerina and their *chagrin d'amour*. In the tale both are consumed by fire, and the metaphorical message of this unassuming story—passion to fire to ashes—is universal. Balanchine's ballet is unclear as to the story and, thus, somewhat dehumanized. Essentially, he uses the plot for an extensive pas de deux; the fairy tale is rendered only vaguely. Without the help of a libretto, it is not apparent to the audience that the ballerina has been blown into the hearth by the wind and burned, and that only the tin heart remains as a memento. Then, too, Bizet's gallop hardly fits the delicate, paper-doll suffering of the pair.

Baryshnikov, along with very few other dancers in contemporary ballet, can embody this sort of toy suffering, this miniaturization of human suffering; we sympathize since it returns us to our childish pity for the inanimate objects that were so like living creatures to us. Balanchine's *Soldier* is a ballet without sentiment, but Baryshnikov supplied it in his execution. He brought warmth to the angular, mechanistic movements that are more graphic than danceable. His face was flatly associated with Petrouchka, and imparted a dense emotional coloration to the soldier—especially via television on March 7, 1979. But again, after *Petrouchka*, a tragic symphony on the same theme, the piece looked like a naïve and trivial scherzo. Immediately, the question was asked: Why do it? After all, you don't let a brilliant Giselle dance her mother, or a Moyna, one of Myrtha's vengeful confidantes.

Baryshnikov's appearance, in *Orpheus* evoked dismay among his admirers. Memorable in the history of the company and innovative for 1948, thirty years later *Orpheus* definitely hadn't benefited from storage. Baryshnikov's casting, or rather miscasting, in it only underscored the untimely character of the revival. Baryshnikov was used as little more than a prop on the stage—solemnly immobile, reluctantly breaking into some miming or would-be dancing as was Balanchine's whim. This waste of talent increased the audience's bitterness to a point where many were ready to share the strong opinion of Barton Wimble in the New York *Daily News*:

> Only one thought remained after seeing Mikhail Baryshnikov do three new roles in three nights with NYCB: Get the hell out!
>
> I had seen him do his first American *Prodigal Son* with the Chicago Ballet two years ago and felt it was a natural role for him. Yet after undoubtedly studying the role with Balanchine himself, his dancing was almost, but not quite, as good, and his total command of the role seems inferior. More than that, his concentration seemed to flag when he was not directly involved, something I thought was impossible in a performer with his stage presence. *Donizetti Variations* gave him an ample opportunity to exhibit his magnetic technique, but here again he seemed to be at a loss with Patricia McBride . . .

Baryshnikov refused to discuss his obvious miscasting even with his

phony in C, with Heather Watts (top) / JOYCE JAFFE *The Four Temperaments* /
THA SWOPE

The Four Temperaments / MARTHA SWOPE

closest friends, as if implying that this kind of hard price for his artistic curiosity was stipulated by the rules of the game.

Small imperfections, inconceivable in his case, marred his dancing in another group of Balanchine's ballets—*Symphony in C, Donizetti Variations, The Four Temperaments*, among them—which presented Baryshnikov in Balanchine's crystallized classicism. As a part of perfectly designed ensemble ballets, such as *Symphony in C* and *The Four Temperaments*, he only demonstrated the discrepancy between his potential and the choreography. His participation was undermined to such an extent that he lost his unique brilliance. His radiant personality appeared muted, and oddly enough, his mind seemed to be more on technical survival than on anything else. In *Symphony in C* he suddenly found himself off balance, which was puzzling considering his perfect coordination. Now and then in *Donizetti Variations* he would lose the timing the part called for. These jarring shortcomings, which he had never revealed before, demanded some explanation.

In my view, they resulted from the clash of two different schoolings. The breakneck speed with which the dense movements were to be performed in *Symphony in C* or in *Donizetti Variations* precluded the classical goal of precision in executing each step. By virtue of his impeccable classical training, Baryshnikov was conditioned to work only this way. The strain on his muscles was so enormous that he would have to dance sloppily from the classical standpoint to keep up with the rhythm. But any kind of imprecision was beyond the ken of his usual muscular reactions. He couldn't help using the classical approach, which resulted in awkwardness.

This collision of two different technical approaches was itself painfully felt in *A Midsummer Night's Dream*. On the one hand, Baryshnikov gave a personal characterization of Oberon as a mischievous, self-confident "chevalier servant," coldly estimating each move in his amorous game to tame his coy lady, Titania. When relaxing on the stage, he dominated it by his imposing presence. On the other hand, Oberon's variation, which is one of the technically insurmountable stumbling blocks in Balanchine's male repertory, obviously baffled Misha: his ankle muscles couldn't get over the arduous transition from a series of turns to the string of split-like jumps. Their execution required a specific Balanchinesque training that was impossible to master in a few months. It is no coincidence that only in Tchaikovsky's

Pas de Deux, whose choreographic patterns are akin to Petipa's pure technique, did Baryshnikov raise the fireworks of his usual virtuosity.

La Sonnambula, Balanchine's most aesthetic ballet, is the only one whose rare unity of color, decor, costumes, and choreography evokes the Diaghilev Seasons at their high point. Dorothea Tanning's costumes and the scenic design are a tribute to the aesthetic principles of Diaghilev's *The World of Art*. The greens of Constantine Somov's paintings, the blue of Léon Bakst, Serge Soudeikine's browns and beiges set one another off marvelously. And the naïve manner of sketching the romantic story—the poet and his dreams, feminine jealousy and revenge, the subsequent death of the poet—corresponds beautifully to the pastoral, slightly plaintive music of Bellini.

Sonnambula, with Patricia McBride / MARTHA SWOPE

La Sonnambula is a ballet of romantic masks, and Baryshnikov's role is basically one of pantomime, but pantomime unlike that in *Orpheus,* where the absence of dance is perceived as a vexing miscalculation. Here, dance would be out of place, disrupting the proportions of the stylization of the old Romantic ballet with its minimization of the male dance. Baryshnikov (as the poet) is utilized in the duet only as a partner in the lifts, but Balanchine's treatment of this role is masterful. The piece is built on the headlong *pas de bourrée* that alternately slows down and rushes ahead in La Sonnambula's racing with the candle, recalling for the audience Pavlova's romantic *pas de bourrée* in *The Dying Swan.*

La Sonnambula is one of Baryshnikov's favorite Balanchine works, because it gave him the opportunity to realize his stylistic sensibility and potential as an actor. He approached the role as that of a pastoral Werther. In dark-beige camisole and brown tights he was a balletic Werther marvelously integrated into the ensemble—a parade of Romantic masks. He understood the stylized nature of the ballet and did not philosophize or weigh his hero down with psychological details. It is perhaps unfortunate that he danced *La Sonnambula* with McBride, a ballerina-ingenue for whom balletic Romanticism is inappropriate. Suzanne Farrell would have been more suitable, or Allegra Kent, an incomparable sleepwalker who created a furor in Leningrad in 1962 and whose approach was close to Baryshnikov's.

At the New York City Ballet Baryshnikov continued the fruitful collaboration with Jerome Robbins that had begun at American Ballet Theatre with Robbins's one-act version of *Other Dances,* choreographed for Misha and Natalia Makarova. Both excelled in this seemingly plotless composition, the most lyrical piece Misha had ever performed in the West.

Oddly enough, the Robbins repertoire has more affinity than Balanchine's with the individual qualities of many great Russian dancers. Makarova considers his ballets less "geometric" and more emotionally colored; Maya Plisetskaya simply views him as "the most refined Russian choreographer in American ballet"; Baryshnikov shares Plisetskaya's enthusiasm. The Robbins repertoire, indeed, gives more scope to the accents with which Misha usually orchestrates his dancing; he values the particular ease in Robbins's patterns, his musicality, and the hidden dramatic tension that has to be revealed through the dancing.

◁ Rehearsing *Other Dances* with Jerome
Robbins / MARTHA SWOPE

With the City Ballet Baryshnikov performed *Other Dances, Dances at a Gathering, Fancy Free, The Four Seasons,* and *Opus 19*. In *Other Dances* his partner was Patricia McBride, who barely matched him in general, and in the Robbins ballets in particular. The contrast of their personal styles in *Other Dances*—her aloofness alongside his impetuosity and humor—was so striking that it tempted one to rename the ballet *Other Dancers*. The poetry of understatement, which distinguished the Makarova-Baryshnikov partnership in this particular ballet, vanished without a trace, paralyzing Baryshnikov. As a result, *Other Dances* seemed to be not so much "a ballet of fire and ice" as an exercise in neoclassical style, set to Chopin's music.

As for *Dances at a Gathering*, a perfect example of the ensemble existential ballet, Baryshnikov's stylistically impeccable characterization was somehow lost in the performance, diminshed by the many inappropriate castings, and interpreted in a low key.

Possibly the most radiant portrayal in terms of the old Robbins repertoire was Baryshnikov's spry and sprightly tar as the second sailor in *Fancy Free*, presented once at the School of American Ballet performance in the spring of 1979. It became a parade of Baryshnikov's hilarious exuberance and stunning technique, transforming a minor role into a miniature masterpiece.

Two ballets, *The Four Seasons* and *Opus 19*, were designed by Robbins for Baryshnikov. The fact that the choreographer turned to the ballet divertissement from Verdi's *Les Vêpres Siciliennes* for a new work, *The Four Seasons*, puzzled many people. This is far from Verdi's best music for ballet from what is far from his best opera. That the music is brisk and quite danceable and structured in four parts hardly guarantees its appeal as ballet. If the phases of the year attracted Robbins, the *Seasons* of Alexander Glazunov are much more interesting. Anna Pavlova and Mikhail Mordkin created an enduring autumn *Bacchanale* to this music.

Robbins was not the first to choreograph the music from Verdi's *Les Vêpres Siciliennes*. A version premièred in 1855 at the Paris Opera House under the aegis of Marius Petipa's brother Lucien. In 1973 Makarova danced Serge Lifar's *The Seasons of the Year* in Turin, in the production of *Les Vêpres Siciliennes* directed by Maria Callas and Giuseppe di Stefano. Makarova's dancing was described by Callas as "the only good thing that I've seen on this stage." Now it was Baryshnikov's turn to dress up Verdi's divertissement, this time via a ballet

Fancy Free / MARTHA SWOPE

that smacks of a Broadway show and brings to mind Jerome Robbins's earliest work.

Robbins himself seemed to be somewhat unsure of his own attitude toward the choreography, judging by a curious eclecticism of both the balletic lexicon and the emotional coloration. On the one hand, there was the traditional theatricality—Janus leading four draped allegorical figures onto the boards one by one, each accompanied by a suite. On the other hand, there was the ironic tone of the Winter segment, with its shivering ballerinas and burlesque devices, and the neutral emotional key in which Spring and Summer were served up. Some sort of definition was given only to Autumn—at least its bacchanalian frenzy was strictly dictated by the music.

Baryshnikov, as Bacchus or a "bacchant," dressed in an unflattering grape-colored mini-tunic, was the central figure of the bacchanalia. The choreography was created especially for Baryshnikov, though his understudy, Peter Martins, danced a different version composed with an eye to his particular qualifications. With the conventions of a musical show in mind, Robbins utilized Baryshnikov as a stunt man, capi-

The Four Seasons / MARTHA SWOPE

talizing on his tremendous vitality and technique. The frenzied orgy of bacchantes dashing about intentionally harked back to Leonid Lavrovsky's *Walpurgisnacht*, which had long since fallen into disrepute in Russia. Baryshnikov had never danced Lavrovsky's piece, but Vasiliev and Plisetskaya, dancers of his caliber, had, with gusto and irony. It is possible that Robbins decided to give Baryshnikov the chance to demonstrate how this sort of *mauvais genre* could be danced seriously today. The dancers of the New York City Ballet tried as hard as they could to reproduce bacchanalian madness; but the exhibitionism of the autumn orgy, exuding licentiousness, was hardly second nature to dancers brought up in the strict puritanical atmosphere of Balanchine's classicism.

Against the background of this mimicry of a bacchanalia, Baryshnikov looked like an alien being, demonstrating the miracles of his technique and, simultaneously, his own Russian irony toward the endless cascade of tricks. As for the variety of dizzying turns and leaps, Baryshnikov had not shown off the like since the Kirov's *Creation of the World*. He unveiled a whole encyclopedia of his unique grand pirouettes, with knee bent in every attitude, and with *sautés* on his working leg. At times he would freeze in the middle of a pirouette, *à la seconde*, and then continue spinning. This was the apotheosis of concentrated speed and flawlessness in the best tradition of the "show stoppers" that marked his parts on the stage of ABT. However, the Nabokovian "dual vision" came through in Baryshnikov's delivery. He seemed to be saying: "See, I can do it this way and that. I can spin like a top; I can stop suddenly or I can keep these pranks coming." Perhaps Baryshnikov didn't share Robbins's belief that this parade of virtuosity with its allusions to a Russian past could be taken seriously.

More appropriately, Robbins created *Opus 19* for Baryshnikov, utilizing the dancer's gift for mastering new elements. In keeping with the choreographer's favored and quite successful genre of existential ballet, *Opus 19* was unique to Baryshnikov's fifteen-month stay with the New York City Ballet in that it was created to take advantage of his development.

Robbins's reading of Prokofiev's violin concerto was iconoclastic without complete justification. The music, one would think, calls for simple, lyrical choreographic resolutions. Instead, the choreography was loaded with references to the ballets of Balanchine and of Robbins himself. The patterns referred to the scuttling insect men from Balanchine's *Kammermusik* or to the hellenistic plasticity of the torsos and arms in *Apollo*. The pert, powerful front thrusts of the legs recalled "Rubies." The figure disappearing into a web of branching arms smacked of *The Dybbuk*. Even the male protagonist victimized by carnivorous predators evoked recollections of *The Cage*. The Slavic references, such as heels digging into the ground or arms thrust akimbo at the hips, corresponding to the Russian tunes in the concerto, came from *Dances at a Gathering* or *Other Dances*.

But the clear references and self-references, for which it is just as easy to reproach Balanchine and Petipa, are quite forgivable in *Opus 19*. Here these features are subordinated to the logic of the existential ballet. As frequently happens with Robbins, *Opus 19* seems, superficially, to lack content. But the dancer's individuality eventually belies unity, giving focus to the diffuse, while implying a universally tragic content. Robbins's ballets are immersed in the poetics of alienation. He requires individuality more than Balanchine does, because impersonality is uncongenial to the alienated characters in his existential ballets. Whereas Balanchine uses graphic metaphors for purely visual effect or intellectual stimulation, Robbins's choreography absorbs the drama of mood, and his dancers are bound to reveal it.

Opus 19 submerges the audience in the twilight world of the unconscious. The protagonist is tormented by painful erotic experiences, sorrow, alienation from a world inhabited by his faceless doubles, hostility from the opposite sex—a whole collection of existential clichés. It is quite appropriate that Baryshnikov, as the protagonist, is stripped to the bare essentials—a skin-hugging T-shirt and tights even paler than his own flesh. In no other ballet—not at ABT, not at the City Ballet—did Baryshnikov look so blatantly athletic. The suppleness and power of his muscles were almost obtrusive in the movements of his strong arms, in the quivering of his torso, in his elastic leaps, which constantly changed direction, in the crisp whirlwind of his turning. His movements seemed to imply a kind of invisible drama, one of sexual identity in which the conflict is merely sketched out. Baryshnikov is placed against the background of the six couples of the corps—faceless beings, who are, in a way, the protagonist's doubles. By accompanying, echoing, or counterpointing the protagonist's movements, they portend the idea of their unity, as if their reality exists mainly through him.

The protagonist's solo with the corps reinforces the impression of a vicious circle in whose confines all of them are irrevocably placed. The

idea of exit is brought out in the pas de deux with a woman in midnight blue. It is not so important whether she is real or a figment of the protagonist's imagination. She is a metaphor of female destructiveness, enduring in his mind.

The pas de deux, structured as a furious struggle of two spiders seemingly devouring each other, helped Baryshnikov reveal new qualities as a dancer. Grabbing his partner from behind in a brutal bear hug, or swinging her around, her legs flung straight out in front, or dropping his head on her spine, his arms and legs surrounding her, Baryshnikov never infused emotional coloration into his movements. The dramatic tension never resulted from an emphasis on superb technical skill or pure theatricality, as it had before. His virtuosity seemed tamed, even understated; it was subjugated to the purely intellectual control that had come to the fore while he was assimilating Balanchine's style. But with Balanchine this special control held his body back without making its potential obvious, without serving any dramatic purpose. *Opus 19* was as free from traditional theatrical vehicles as any of Balanchine's creations, but the added dimension of drama was realized through pure dance language. Baryshnikov's brooding virtuosity, expressed only by his body, extended the content of this vague drama.

On October 12, 1979, Baryshnikov danced the role of the Poet in *La Sonnambula* at the Kennedy Center in Washington, D.C. It turned out to be his last appearance with the New York City Ballet.

The reasons for his resignation were various, but certainly a dangerous physical condition consisting of tendonitis and other injuries did not account for it. The invitation to become the artistic director of ABT beginning in 1980 arrived unexpectedly, but at an opportune time. From July 1978 to October 1979 he had performed twenty-two new roles, an achievement worthy of a dance career extended beyond retirement age.

Balanchine's techniques undoubtedly increased his physical potential by developing his coordination and, most important, by reinforcing his intellectual attitude toward dancing. His attempt to extend the boundaries of his Russian experience was mostly successful. But Misha was no longer able to carry on, because Balanchine's style began to take its toll on his body.

His physical conditioning was a perfect product of Petipa's technique. Petipa was concerned with stamina, creating for dancers who had to perform his full-length ballets. And his choreography is the most logical and comfortable to perform, even if it demands energy. Misha's body, conditioned for Petipa's marathon, was seriously risked in Balanchine's sprint-like balletic elements. The technique of beats and jumps, fashioned after Bournonville's standards, jeopardized his soaring *ballon*. He was becoming more stocky and muscular, losing his flexibility and his legato-like flowing movements. For fifteen months he experimented with his body and artistry, playing with fire. A peripheral concern was the possibility that his prestige as an exemplar of classical dance would suffer in the eyes of the public, and that in the Balanchine-Baryshnikov duel he would be a winner with losses.

At the outset of Misha's career in the West, Arlene Croce incisively wrote: "The feeling he leaves you with is one of intense pleasure mingled with the ache of frustration . . . Every performance confirms his potential, and part of the anguish we feel comes from the fear that his potential may be wasted. He harbors the future, but his roles keep him from exploring it." In view of Misha's experience with the City Ballet, Croce's words acquired a special meaning. Balanchine's placing him in Edward Villella's repertory as a *demi-caractère* dancer precluded the proper employment of his pure classicism: Baryshnikov never danced *Divertimento 15*, "Diamonds," *Raymonda Variations*, *Ballo della Regina*, or, with the City Ballet, *Theme and Variations*. *Orpheus*, with its static patterns, and *The Four Temperaments*, a masterpiece of ensemble ballet in which Bart Cook looked as convincing as Baryshnikov, and the leftovers from the Russian imperial banquet, such as *Harlequinade* and *The Steadfast Tin Soldier*, never made demands on Baryshnikov's full technique and artistry.

This misuse of Baryshnikov was somehow overlooked by Anna Kisselgoff, who reviewed his taxing experience with the City Ballet in *The New York Times*. She regarded the way Baryshnikov was cast or miscast as a triumph of the aesthetic principles of Balanchine: "The chief lesson of the Baryshnikov experience then is not so much what it showed about Mikhail Baryshnikov, but what it proved about the New York City Ballet. It is, as some people refuse to believe, a creative institution so strongly molded by the Balanchine esthetic that no single star—not even a Russian superstar—could hope to make a dent in its artistic profile. Nor should any dancer do so." Moreover, Balanchine's

"I don't create for anybody" seems to evoke enthusiasm in the critic. The democratic approach of a company without stars—its orientation around the ensemble—and Balanchine's actual choreographic practices are two different things that Kisselgoff arbitrarily linked together. It is no secret to anyone that major dancers in the troupe, such as Suzanne Farrell and Peter Martins, as well as past artists such as Edward Villella, Arthur Mitchell, Allegra Kent, and Maria Tallchief, were no less important than Balanchine's ballets themselves, quite apart from the fact that the old pleiad departed and the ballets remained. And several of the ballets suffer precisely from the absence of the right cast. After Villella and Baryshnikov, who is up to dancing *The Prodigal Son*? Who is there to replace Allegra Kent in *La Sonnambula*? Or Gelsey Kirkland in *Theme and Variations*? After all, even if Balanchine's company is his instrument, with him as composer and conductor, it's not a matter of indifference whether it is a Steinway or a piano of Soviet manufacture.

Between a brilliant dancer and a brilliant choreographer there is no question of priority, for one cannot exist without the other. The names of Pavlova and Nijinsky are not overshadowed by the names of Petipa, Perrot, or Bournonville in the history of ballet. And today Balanchine will have to share his indisputable glory with Martins, Farrell, and others, as he did formerly with André Eglevsky, Tanaquil LeClercq, and Maria Tallchief.

In connection with Baryshnikov's presence in the New York City Ballet, Anna Kisselgoff wrote in *The New York Times*:

> It is no secret that Mr. Baryshnikov's star presence was never as strong in the City Ballet as it was in the Ballet Theatre or other companies. But this, too, was to be expected, with Mr. Balanchine predicting that audiences looking for the show-stopping "tricks" of Mr. Baryshnikov's 19th century roles would be disappointed simply because his own choreography did not allow for them.

Contrary to Balanchine's claims, some of his male roles (in *Donizetti Variations* or Oberon's variation in *A Midsummer Night's Dream*, for instance) are much more effective and "show-stopping" than any of Petipa's or Perrot's creations, whether those of Siegfried, Prince

Florimund, or Albrecht. The latter look like childish nonsense when compared with Balanchine's devilishly subtle combinations, which occasionally endanger the dancer's body, taking it close to the breaking point. (It isn't necessary to mention the female roles, whose highly concentrated, taxing dancing is perfectly apparent throughout Balanchine's ballets.)

Of course, had Baryshnikov joined the City Ballet at twenty rather than thirty, his entire experience would have been different. But with Balanchine, Baryshnikov would hardly have remained the well-rounded master he is, a dancer who is at home in all balletic styles. The theater of Balanchine is one of narrow specialization, something that his dancers, bewitched by his refined innovations, perhaps do not understand. They may think that the transition from *Symphony in C* to *Giselle* or *Swan Lake* is as easy as two times two, but, in practice, it doesn't happen that way. Peter Martins, for instance, who is steeped in the school of Bournonville and Balanchine, is superb in *La Sylphide* and somewhat lost in *Swan Lake*, which demands adherence to the style of Petipa and Ivanov, the conventions of pantomime, large, swooping movements on stage—all that is hostile to Balanchine's aesthetics.

Psychologically, working with Balanchine helped Misha understand how sharply the Russian classical school and its spiritual heir, Balanchine, diverge—their resemblance is no greater than that of grandfather and grandson. And the myth of an ideal Maryinsky Theater that Baryshnikov cherished in his heart turned out to be, in fact, pure invention. A half year after leaving Balanchine, when the petty hurts no longer colored Baryshnikov's undoubtedly noble experiment, he said to me, "I'll never regret that I worked with him. He is a great man and a great choreographer. And I think that he deflated certain of my fantasies about myself while helping me to acquire greater confidence in my field."

What is more, it's possible that, if he hadn't gone through Balanchine's school—even at such breakneck speed—Misha wouldn't have wanted to accept the position of artistic director at ABT and wouldn't have considered new works as a choreographer. And when he begins to choreograph ballets at ABT, possibly Misha's *éducation sentimentale* with Balanchine and his incredibly imaginative work will be reflected in his own works. His control has grown, and in all his future experiments the experience with Balanchine will be with him. Balanchine helped Baryshnikov progress; he grew in the choreographer's company, as a person and as an artist. And if everything did not go smoothly—that's the usual cost of the educational process.

THE YEAR 1979 was a crucial and exciting one in Baryshnikov's life. In the spring he flew to Yale University to receive an honorary doctorate of fine arts. Because of foggy weather in New Haven, Misha's plane was diverted to Bridgeport. He had to be rushed to the campus by police escort, arriving barely in time to hear Yale president A. Bartlett Giamatti declare: "You have brought classical dance to millions as you made your *grands jetés* into their lives. With the courage of your conviction that artistic growth demands adventure, you have dared to let 'push come to shove' as you moved from Petipa to Tharp and Balanchine."

Trips to Buenos Aires that summer, to London with the City Ballet in September, and to Paris for a short season became the coda of Misha's relatively brief Balanchine period, marking the beginning of a short respite from classical ballet.

During this period he also traveled to China (July 1979), for the Bob Hope television special, where he danced Act II from *Giselle* and gave master classes. His personal report on China, far more illuminating than the show, was tinged equally with sadness about the situation in China and enthusiasm regarding its dancers: "They are very gifted. They have soft muscles, an innate *plié*, and that special Oriental flexibility, combined with the capacity to grasp your instructions. Teaching them was a delight. Maybe in the future they will be able to overcome a certain provincialism that marks their manner of presentation. As for their life, it was a real anti-nostalgia pill. My God, it resembles Russia so much: misery and scarcity, though they have enough food and the local KGB pressure is milder. They are allowed to talk to foreigners much more freely than in Russia, and can even enter the hotels. Their tongues are less tied. But the present is drab in comparison with the glorious Chinese past, hopelessly looking at you through the eyes of the ancient palaces, magnificent pagodas. I brought back to New York some old theater costumes; they are sold to the tourists the same way the icons were once sold in Russia for foreign currency . . ."

On his way back to New York he stayed for a short time in Tokyo, where the Kirov company was on tour. Incognito, he saw the "Kingdom of the Shades" and *Giselle*, but avoided meeting his former colleagues. It would have been a frustrating experience. He wouldn't be able to say how devastatingly gray the company looked despite the efforts of Oleg Vinogradov to brush up the corps and orient it to the old noble style. Something has been lost for good, and now the ABT ballerinas perform the "Shades" much better than their counterparts at the place of origin. New talents were not apparent, and the veterans revealed their fatigue. In many ways these revelations marked the end of the Kirov legend for Misha. From a car window he saw some of the Kirov dancers strolling around a Tokyo street, and he sent them his silent greetings. He treated them as strangers, though he was not afraid of inflicting KGB fury upon them. By all reports, the KGB adheres to a new policy of instructing the Kirov dancers not to flee from the great Russian defectors but to demonstrate the escalation of freedom in Russia. For Misha this new flexibility was of no importance, since his emotional ties with the Kirov had been severed for good. Only the cultural links still persist—the Maryinsky-Kirov at its prime remains for him an ideal model of classical dance.

When Baryshnikov accepted the offer to take over the American Ballet Theatre as artistic director beginning in September 1980, the news of his appointment produced an upheaval of sorts in balletic circles. Baryshnikov will be just thirty-two when he inherits this empire of eighty-seven dancers and seventy-five ballets from Lucia Chase and Oliver Smith (who have been co-directors since 1945). Since he is at the peak of his artistry, many feel that it is too early for him to burden his career as a dancer with the responsibilities of management.

After his experiment with Balanchine, Misha may be motivated by a new ambition: if Balanchine created a neoclassical ballet based loosely on Petipa and popular American dance culture, why not return to the source now and re-create the pure classics on American soil? Why not reshape the company on the model of the Kirov in the days of its undisputed glory? ABT has tremendous potential, but the management has grown older, and the dancers have been left without guidance, to develop or languish on their own. Baryshnikov's experience with ABT during his staging of *The Nutcracker* and *Don Quixote* was stimulating—the company's performance of the Spanish-flavored choreography of *Don Quixote* seemed especially promising. Of course, one cannot expect miracles. The Maryinsky-Kirov was nurtured for a century and a half, and Baryshnikov must attempt to go through the same process in a matter of years. The main thing for Baryshnikov will be to teach the ABT dancers to be stylists—to dance *Giselle*, a Romantic ballet, differently from *Swan Lake* and *The Sleeping Beauty*, the culminations of academic dance.

Swan Lake will most likely be the first ballet he tackles. So far he's not sure what approach he'll take to this Petipa-Ivanov jewel, which has been framed and chiseled in various ways over a hundred years. He is still hesitating whether to return to its original fairy-tale form or present its modernized version as a psychological drama. However that may be, he said in interviews in *Newsweek* and *Time*: "In the classics are my strength and my training . . . I will find new choreographers. I do not intend to use ABT as some training ground for myself . . . In a way, I will be onstage every night—if a ballerina does not do 32 fouettés, then I will feel that I have failed too. In fact, if you put on a ballet that calls for 32 fouettés, you should have a ballerina who can do 46 . . ."

Baryshnikov doesn't regard ABT as a stage to sweep, but as "a beautiful Tiffany lamp, made from many wonderful pieces of glass. What can I say? Some parts of the lamp are missing . . .

"There have been so many things in my life, so many risky positions, tricky situations, so many premières and styles. I did not know what could excite me after all that, but this does. Probably, I sound like anyone who ever started a publishing house or a restaurant. You always think you can do better."

After Misha parted company with Balanchine, he spent two weeks relaxing in the Caribbean, only to return and give his friends a new jolt. He accepted an invitation to take part in another TV special—the Gary Smith–Dwight Hemion production, *Baryshnikov on Broadway*. It was conceived as Baryshnikov's personal tribute to one of America's great traditions, and Misha wanted to be assisted by Liza Minnelli. As she said: "Misha just called me and said people wanted him to do a TV special and would I do it with him, and I said: 'Yeah, I would love to do it. It would be thrilling to be able to work with you.' "

Misha's choice was not as puzzling as it seemed to many. To him it would be the realization of a childhood dream. He first saw American musicals with Gene Kelly, Fred Astaire, and his all-time hero, James Cagney, at the cinema in Riga. As Misha recalled in an interview for the New York *Daily News*: "I just couldn't believe that somebody could dance, sing, act, tap—all at the same time. When I finally went on tour to other countries with the Kirov company, I was exposed to much more of the American style, and I grew jealous. I kept asking myself why I couldn't do that!" The first time he saw Cagney films

Baryshnikov on Broadway
/ MARTHA SWOPE

was in the mid-fifties. As he recalled in an interview in *After Dark*: "I would stand in line for eight hours to get a ticket . . . Cagney had a special appeal for me. This guy could dance in one movie and then in the next his fist was there and the fellow was on the floor. It was quite unbelievable. I knew his name before I knew Fred Astaire's name. Fred Astaire was sort of untouchable—not very close to reality somehow. Cagney was often a gangster, always fighting against somebody and it was very real. In a funny way, he was one of the first big influences on me, so when I met him so many years later, it was great." (Misha met his screen hero in the autumn of 1979.)

Misha kept the content of the show secret—in the Russian manner, so as not to put a hex on it. From his brief remarks I learned that since

In Connecticut, with Gennady Smakov and Alexander Godunov / DOMINIQUE NABOKOV

November 1979 he had been practicing tap dancing six hours at a time. In response to my question about whether or not it was difficult, he said: "Very. It's not improvisation at all, as many assume in Russia, with the body just responding to the rhythm and jumping about in all directions. There's a completely different feeling of control in tap—much sharper than in classical dance."

At the beginning Misha was far from being sure of his success in so different a domain. Choreographer Ron Field was also apprehensive about working with a dancer of Misha's caliber. Only after Field's customary two-to-three-week period of "testing the limitations" was he reassured. As he said in an interview in *The New York Times*: "I'd worked with other male ballet dancers and it was like 'Get down, Danilova.' It never came out jazz or at ease . . . The dancers tend to present the insides of their thighs and also there's an attitude that ballet demands that makes the dancers, when they try to get jazzy, corny and like hep-cats. So I'm stretching Misha in areas where he never dreamed he'd have to send messages—to his hips, his knees, and his shoulders. And he adores it! And he loves hearing himself dance, like in tap . . . I realized there were no limits with Misha. I could really turn him into a Donald O'Connor or a Gene Kelly or a Ray Bolger. He has that facility. His body is not rigidly set in classical ballet, and he's able to send messages to his hips and chest and all—just like a Broadway dancer."

In November, both were reassured that the show would get off the ground. Sometime in December, while we were both in Connecticut, Misha dropped by for a drink and, to my amazement, played me a tape with him and Liza singing hits such as "Sunrise, Sunset" and "Shall We Dance." Commenting on the collaboration, Misha said: "Liza's great. She is so helpful, patient, cooperative. It's a pleasure to work with her."

The tape conveyed the feeling of rehearsal. Liza corrected his pronunciation and rhythm (". . . It's *joint*, like *oi*"), and you could hear them laughing and joking. Previously, I had heard Misha playing the piano and singing the songs of the "unofficial" Soviet *chansonniers*, Bulat Okudzhava and Vladimir Vysotsky, his late friend. It was nice on an amateur level—musical, but no more. But this time I was struck by how free his voice sounded. It seemed incredible coming from a Soviet dancer born in Riga, who grew up in the puritanical atmosphere of Leningrad and for whom Broadway's subculture had been as distant as the moon. I couldn't help but express my amazement, and this pleased Misha. He jumped up, singing the words and "jiving" to the music, enjoying it all in an almost childlike way.

The tape was a surprise for James Cagney, whom we'd soon be seeing at a dinner party given by Milos Forman. That evening Cagney, his wife, and the couple that look after them arrived at the Formans' last. The eighty-year-old Cagney, who is nicely plump for his age and moves about with difficulty, spent most of the evening in an armchair. Only the characteristic ironic smile playing on his thin lips gave away the former tough guy of the American movies of the thirties and forties. Misha started his tape with "Give My Regards to Broadway" from *Yankee Doodle Dandy*. Cagney smiled. Misha started dancing in front of him, and his hero mumbled: "Not bad, honest to God, not bad!"

Misha was as happy as a kid.

After dinner we all watched *Yankee Doodle Dandy*, which Milos had brought along with him to Connecticut from New York. Cagney warned us in advance, half-joking, half-serious: "The dialogue is ridiculous and it's not particularly interesting when I'm playing a scene—but the dancing is a different matter." He is truly magnificent in this film from the forties, the ideological message and even the editing of which recall certain Soviet films of the same period. "I don't know who stole from whom," Misha remarked to me after the movie, "but the film could have come from Mosfilm, judging by the manner of execution." Misha was right, in that Soviet musical comedies of the thirties *were* cut from an American pattern. American directing, scriptwriting, and sound tracks were raided. Thanks to the iron curtain of the time, no one was in a position to object.

The hour-long ABC-TV special *IBM Presents Baryshnikov on Broadway* (April 24, 1980) excited as many Baryshnikov fans as it perplexed and disappointed. Those who were looking forward to seeing a reincarnation of Fred Astaire thought the show too banal and even degrading for Misha. Others wondered why this unique virtuoso of classical ballet would lower himself to a "cheap genre." One opinion I heard was even stronger: "Next time we'll be given the opportunity to watch Baryshnikov munching on popcorn."

The show itself didn't shatter my expectations because I hadn't dreamed of being treated to a new *Gay Divorcee*. Fred Ebb's script, which turned corny at times—especially when Liza arrived with a pastrami on rye with Russian dressing!—had, seemingly, no other pur-

At home in Connecticut, with
Gennady Smakov / DOMINIQUE NAB

pose than pure entertainment. The journey through the studio's looking glass, with Misha as a kind of Alice led by Liza into the wonderland of musicals, never exceeded the proportions of garishness or tacky exuberance which are endemic to this kind of show. As such, *Baryshnikov on Broadway* passes as a competent American television musical.

Ron Field, the choreographer, explained in *Dance Magazine*: "I wanted to celebrate Broadway, but without using cartoon copies of other people's choreography." He seemed to be mostly concerned with evoking the essence of each style. Every number, from the "Honeysuckle Rose" duet with the ravishing Nell Carter, to the finale from *A Chorus Line*, was as buoyant and legitimate as it was unimaginative.

Because the program was assembled from a wide variety of musicals—*Guys and Dolls, Cabaret, Fiddler on the Roof* and *Can Can* among them—Baryshnikov was faced with the task of impersonating many styles, without having expertise in any of them. Some numbers were unsuited to him. The opening suite from *Oklahoma!* is obtrusively dated, and led Baryshnikov to overact in order to bring the conventional cowboy mask to life. The show's fragmentary nature, its lack of a narrative, made it impossible for Baryshnikov to excel as both dancer and actor. He was commissioned to be an impersonator, and his performance in this show should be measured, not against the mastery of Fred Astaire, but against himself as a classical dancer. In this respect what he has achieved seems to be unparalleled in ballet annals. As John J. O'Connor wrote in *The New York Times*:

> Mr. Baryshnikov is extraordinary, not only for his dancing, but also for that indefinable something called presence. He can be boyish without being cute, he can be a star without being overbearing. He performs taps, jazz, comic and period dancing with a dedicated exuberance. In the *Guys and Dolls* number, he manages to evoke a young James Cagney or, more precisely, a Frank Gorshin impersonation of Cagney.

Misha enjoyed every minute of rehearsal and performance. Liza Minnelli reported in *After Dark*: "If he didn't have fun with it, he wouldn't be as good as he is. There is some joy that is absolutely catching when you watch Baryshnikov—besides the fact that he's doing everything perfectly: Jesus Jesse! How-did-that-happen-how-did-he-do-that-what-was-that-again-I-can't-believe-a-human-body-just-did-that! But what lingers in your mind is that somebody really got off on it."

This personal touch, his exuberant involvement in the show, modified the image of unruffled masculinity with which he had imbued his portrayal of a dancer in *The Turning Point*. And when he appeared in the finale of *A Chorus Line*, not as the greatest dancer in the world, but as an ordinary Broadway "gypsy," savoring his joy of dancing and sharing it exuberantly with the audience, the glitter of his costume and his impishly beaming face seemed, in a split second, to illuminate his whole career. I suddenly recalled the eighteen-year-old boy, in garish green harem pants with a silvery aigrette on his forehead, the little slave for *Le Corsaire* spinning out his miraculous grand pirouette on the former imperial stage of the former St. Petersburg. Fifteen years of hard work, inspiration, and achievement had passed for Misha since that unforgettable moment, yet here he was, shining on an American television screen as a kid from a Broadway musical. Another image crossed my mind: in saying goodbye to Cagney at Milos Forman's party, Misha did a marvelous takeoff on Cagney's dancing, tossing his legs about in overlapping figures and sticking his backside out. Remembering his Kirov debut and his recent dance à la Cagney, I could not help but think that his dedicated, flamboyant performance in *Baryshnikov on Broadway* was another significant achievement for him. I wondered where he would go next, where his boundless curiosity would lead him. He will undoubtedly surprise us; I have never ceased expecting the unexpected from him. After all, Baryshnikov left the classical hothouse of the Kirov to revel in artistic freedom in the West. We shall see . . .

 Index